ISBN -13: 978-1-7292-6662-5

1

Table of Contents

WILD WOMEN ON THE ROAD 4

ACKNOWLEDGEMENTS 5

PREFACE 6

CHAPTER ONE: ANSWERING THE WILD CALL TO FREEDOM.. 9

DIG DEEPER: DISCOVER YOUR COMPELLING WHY 26

CHAPTER TWO: FEAR; OUR BIGGEST OBSTACLE 31

DIG DEEPER: HOW TO GET OUT OF THE FEAR TRAP..... 53

CHAPTER THREE: TRUSTING YOUR WILD NATURE TO GUIDE YOU 59

DIG DEEPER: TUNE IN TO YOUR WILD GUIDE – THE BODY COMPASS.. 72

CHAPTER FOUR: NAVIGATING THE ROCKY ROADS OF CHANGE 82

DIG DEEPER: AVOIDING THE PERILS OF GETTING STUCK IN LIMBO-LAND 94

CHAPTER FIVE: NOMADISM AND THE CHALLENGES OF THE HERO'S JOURNEY... 103

DIG DEEPER: GET SUPPORT FOR YOUR HERO'S JOURNEY 120

CHAPTER SIX: DOWNSIZING, PURGING, AND CLEARING, OH MY! 125

DIG DEEPER: TIPS TO KEEP YOUR SANITY DURING THE PURGE.. 140

CHAPTER SEVEN: NOMADISM - A WOMEN'S MOVEMENT 151

DIG DEEPER: EXPLORING YOUR PERSONAL WOMEN'S MOVEMENT 169

CHAPTER EIGHT: NOW FOR A BIT OF THE PRACTICAL STUFF 174

DIG DEEPER: MAKE PLANS FOR YOUR IDEAL DAY AS A NOMAD 191

RESOURCES 193

DEFINITIONS 195

WILD WOMEN ON THE ROAD
A Women's Guide
To Nomadic Freedom In The Modern Age
By Mary Ellen Telesha Certified Life Coach and Nomad.

About the author: Mary Ellen is a Certified Martha Beck Life Coach for Women, Master Level Reiki Practitioner, and Nomad. Before finding her calling as a Women's Life Coach, she worked 20 years as a patient care advocate for Planned Parenthood, an invaluable experience for appreciating the rich and complex lives of women.

Find her on Facebook and Instagram as
@CosmicNomadVoyager.
She writes about her nomad experiences on
Cosmicnomadvoyager.com

ACKNOWLEDGEMENTS

To my children, Janel and Brittany, my other two hearts, who've supported Mom's crazy journey every step of the way, and to Nancy, the love of my life, who never complained once during the seemingly endless months of writing this book. Not only is her infinite patience and love infused into every word, she poured her time into editing the second updated version!

PREFACE

I originally wrote this book in 2018, one year after becoming a nomad. This updated version comes after 6 years of successful full-time nomad life!

During those years I wrote two more books, a companion journal to this book, and designed a journal for outdoor enthusiasts. All found on Amazon:

Companion Journal To Wild Women On The Road

Top Ten Lists For Nomads: A (Mostly) Humorous Look At Nomadic Life

600 Days As A Nomad: How the Mystical Power of Nature Healed My Body, Mind, and Soul

Outdoor Life Creative Journal For Campers, Nature Lovers, Nomads and Wanderers.

During my years on the road I survived a pandemic and the resulting economic fallout in the U.S. You can read more about my experience as a nomad during the pandemic at CosmicNomadVoyager.com/nomad-vs-pandemic/. The pandemic took a toll financially on our society, resulting in an influx of homeless and disadvantaged taking to nomad life. For many, the act of survival outweighed concern for the environment, and the nomad landscape changed for the worst for full-timers out here on the road.

Many free wilderness areas that were previously open to nomads closed due to overuse and garbage dumping, as a new, and more desperate breed of nomad started moving to these areas. Not only that, people going stir crazy during the pandemic looked to outdoor recreation, and many had no outdoor skills or knowledge.

Even with all that, I have continued to be in love with nomad life!

Like a jewel with many facets, the beautiful facets of nomad life reflect the many sides of who we are. As the years go by I've learned to love all the facets of nomad life!

I wrote this book not just for female nomads, but for anyone who needs some inspiration! I've included the life coaching wisdom that changed my life and was instrumental in making my nomad life a success.

If you're reading this, you're probably among the exponentially growing numbers of women feeling the mysterious pull of nomadic life. Whether you're in the dreaming stage, planning stage, or already on the road, you'll relate to the stories in this book and how we live our lives as women. The way you travel doesn't matter, be it in a car, a van, an apartment size RV, or a tent; what matters is that you are a seeker of freedom and authentic way of life.

There are two journeys we take as female nomads, one the physical, encompassing the roads we take, sights we see and fellow nomads we meet, and the other the profound inner journey we take as we discover our wild and untamed selves on the road. Along with my own story and practical information, this book is designed to help you navigate that rich inner journey.

Each chapter is followed by Dig Deeper exercises, worksheets designed to help navigate the sometimes confounding emotional detours that threaten to take us off course in our journeys. The complete volume of exercises in this book can also be found separately on Amazon, in The Companion Journal to Wild Women On The Road.

May you navigate all of your journeys well, wherever you are!

CHAPTER ONE: ANSWERING THE WILD CALL TO FREEDOM

"To find the Wild Woman, it is necessary for women to return to their instinctive lives, their deepest knowing." ~ Clarissa Pinkola Estes PhD

Are you a *Wild Woman?* You are if you *feel in your bones* that there must be more to life than the way you're living. You are if you *crave the liberation* of your most authentic self. You are if you've finally decided that life is too short to spend in misery, and you're *ready to find the freedom and happiness you know is out there waiting for you.*

You crave something different. You want to be real. You're ready to be completely, entirely *free.*

As I've sat over the many months writing this book, my heart has welled up for all the women out there dreaming, planning, or living on the road. You amaze me! I'm only one on this journey, with my partner Nancy we make two, but when I reach out with my heart, there you all are. We are a tribe of Wild Women on the Road, and your spirits are shining.

Individually, we're being drawn to life on the road, but the nomadic movement is a larger vision for all women. Our inward journey is a solitary path, but that larger vision connects us all as a tribe.

Nomadism as a women's movement is one that's once again changing who we are in the world. It's a movement of freedom, and of knowing what we're capable of. Nomadism is teaching us we are so much more than what we've been convinced to believe, that our spirits run deeper than the patriarchy wants us to see. We've known it forever, since the beginning of humanity, and now we're reclaiming that knowledge for ourselves.

In these modern times, the authentic woman is rising again in all her fierceness, and one of the ways she's showing up in the world is in the increasing multitudes of women following the call of their wild hearts to live as nomads. We as women are being called back to Freedom! Freedom and loving closer to nature are often top reasons why a Wild Woman takes to the road. Those are definitely a few of mine.

It's December of 2017, one of those crisp, bright winter mornings on the Arizona desert. When I finally get motivated enough to crawl out of my cozy mini-van, I've layered up in two long sleeve shirts, a heavy hoodie, two pairs of socks, Timberland boots and winter gloves. By the time I've finished my morning coffee-making ritual, the sun is high in the piercing blue sky of the West, warming the sandy earth, the clear desert air, and me. Sitting with the sun at my back and coffee in hand, the sunshine pours down on me, and I absorb its penetrating warmth. The breeze is slight and cool, now a perfect contrast to the rays of heat behind me. A hummingbird, attracted to the tie-dyed colors of my sweatshirt, dives in to hover for a few seconds at eye level, giving me a little start of joy before buzzing off again into the wild. I'm at peace, my heart is full, and as I reflect on the preciousness of life, I feel my body melt in relaxation, welcoming this perfect, tranquil moment. I've spent a good part of my life lacking this joyousness ... now I let this incredible feeling of wellness expand and make a home in my body.

This is a typical morning for me, traveling and living out of my 2005 Chevy Uplander Mini-Van. This is my WHY.

I'm not alone. In the last few years there's been a wave of women from all walks of life, of all ages, ethnic backgrounds, financial means, straight, gay, conservative, liberal and otherwise, who've chosen to leave behind a "normal" life living in "sticks and bricks," (traditional housing) and made the radical decision to live the fantastically non-traditional life of a nomad. For most of us, this means living without the modern conveniences of faucets, flush toilets, refrigerators, or washing machines - in mobile housing that ranges anywhere from as small as a Prius, up to larger vehicles like converted vans, school buses, and RVs ... and for some brave wild women, in tents. Call us nomads, rubber tramps, vagabonds, vagrants, transients, wanderers or wayfarers, we're doing it in all kinds of vehicles in all sorts of styles, from the most simple to the most elegant, in the never-ending variety expressed by the infinite personalities of women on the road.

What In The World Would Ever Possess Us To Do Such A Thing?

If you're reading this book, you're likely a woman thinking about or currently living a nomadic life ... full or part-time ... and the good news is there hasn't been a better time for you. The number of nomads is exploding. -

In January of 2018, the Rubber Tramp Rendezvous, (RTR for short) an annual gathering of nomads out in the Arizona desert, founded and organized by Bob Wells of CheapRVLiving.com, was estimated at over three thousand participants - a dramatic increase from the few dedicated handful of nomads who've gathered in past years. Bob, an experienced van-dweller himself, has worked steadily over the years to bring information to the public on how to live a free nomadic life, and his YouTube channel often features women on the road. His philosophy, and interviews of women, were a major inspiration for my own journey.

While the format of The RTR has changed since then, it remains an opportunity to meet a wide variety of fellow nomads and get educated about the nomadic lifestyle. There's usually updates on solar, food prep, gadgets and other practical topics. The free workshops cover topics of safety, stealth camping, van conversions, how to get mail, finances, hygiene, and as always, the ever popular, how to poop without modern plumbing. Attracting a wide range of humans, there are smaller breakout camps like Art Camp, Meditation Camp, and Music Camp, along with groups organized around vehicle types and other interests. The NY Times did a comprehensive article on the nomadic phenomenon, calling the 2018 RTR "The Real Burning Man." (My partner and I even made it into the article - there's a photograph of us attending one of Bob Wells' workshops, look for the back of my head in a purple hat.) You can find the article online at https://www.nytimes.com/2018/01/31/style/rubber-tramp-rendezvous-rv-trucks-vanlife.html.

The 2018 RTR took place with camping on site, and as with any gathering of that magnitude, there was noise and chaos, but for a such a large group of full-time, part-time, and wanna-be wild nomads, there were minimal problems. Many of the attendees of the 2018 RTR were women who'd made impressive trips from all over the country to attend.

As an adjunct to the RTR is the women's only gathering, the WRTR, short for Women's Rubber Tramp Rendezvous. Suanne Carlson, the director and organizer of the WRTR and now Executive Director of Homes On Wheels Alliance, is a seasoned nomad, women's advocate, and expert in nomadic living. Suanne facilitates a team who make the WRTR a relevant and supportive event for her fellow nomads, and also happens to be one of the impressively successful minimalists who makes her way on the road living in a Prius. As she says in a YouTube video, Women's Rubber Tramp Rendezvous (WRTR) 2019, the goals of the WRTR are "to help women be successful in the vandwelling lifestyle, be they in a car, a van or RV, as well as to build community, so that you make friends, and learn from people that are around you." Current information and upcoming dates for both events can be found on CheapRVLiving.com. and HomesOnWheelsalliance.org, the non-profit organization that grew out of the work of Bob Wells.

Although I found myself overwhelmed at times by the sheer number of attendees of the main RTR in 2018, the smaller women's only WRTR was refreshingly intimate. The workshops were specifically geared towards women's issues, with sessions on safety on the road, managing finances, hygiene, and dealing with stress. There was an optional potluck each evening, an information table that included a contact list of women with specific needs paired by a list of women with specific skills to offer, a community campfire every night, and at both the RTR and WRTR, the popular "Free Pile" where one can donate or take goodies such as clothes, food, electronics and lots of other road-worthy gear. As Suanne describes the WRTR in this video about the 2018 WRTR, the mentoring of women by other women is a core value of WRTR. If you're reading the print version of this book, you can find the YouTube video on Bob Wells CheapRvLiving channel: 2018 Women''s Rubber Tramp Rendezvous (WRTR): Review and Future.

After 8 months on the road, the 2018 WRTR was my first experience with a large gathering of nomadic women. I found the courage and fierceness of every woman I met there awe-inspiring. I felt welcomed and supported among this diverse group of women, and it felt like I'd come home to my tribe on the road. Having lived as an isolated introvert for many years, I hadn't gone on the road looking for community … but to my surprise, this tribe of nomadic women felt like a perfect fit. The Women of the WRTR, as with most nomadic women I've met on the road, share a profound willingness to support and uplift each other in this sometimes intimidating lifestyle; and expressed the best qualities of women: inclusiveness, cooperation, nurturing and mentoring to name a few. If you're a female nomad craving connection and community, you'll definitely want to include this tribe gathering in your wanderings. From there friendships are made and bonds formed that often result in traveling together down the road.

Over the years the formats and location of the WRTR have changed, but the spirit of women still remains the focus and I make room in my travels to attend each one.

So why in this modern age would we ever make the decision to leave behind the material comforts of four walls?

Besides the practical transitions we face, becoming a female nomad in this unconventional life also often includes long periods of time away from family and friends, the sometimes agonizing process of purging material processions, and a willingness to face primal fears, including personal safety, an issue especially relevant to women.

The freedom of this nomadic life doesn't come without a price, and I find it fascinating to consider why so many of us are increasingly drawn to it.

What are we looking for?
Are we running towards life, or running away from it?
Is it by choice, or necessity?
Are we trying to escape ourselves, or find ourselves?

Or are we just crazy? (A question I've asked about myself on a few occasions!)

Finding a sense of freedom is high on the list for many nomadic women, but there are as many diverse reasons to live a mobile lifestyle as there are diverse women. Some women are forced into nomadism out of economic necessity, while for many of us it's by choice. Or it starts out as an economic necessity after a messy divorce, retirement, or other crisis, but then transitions into a cherished way of life.

Besides craving a sense of freedom, other reasons women hit the road include:

To exit a materialistic/consumerist lifestyle.
To travel and see more of the world.
Wanting to live closer to nature.
To escape an unfulfilling life.
To escape themselves.
To escape unhappiness or another undesirable emotional state.
Financial hardship.
To Save Money.
Health reasons, such as mold exposure/illness.
Feeling of control.

Empowerment.
Hiding from someone or something.
Wanting to live authentically.
Wanting to find a like-minded community.
To heal physically.
To heal emotional turmoil or trauma.
To live a more meaningful life.
Wanting to LIVE before we die.

The old structures that have shaped women's lives for centuries are slowly crumbling, and women are coming alive to their authentic nature. Currently we're experiencing a pushback on civil and women's rights, but more than ever *women are craving freedom and a life unrestrained by a society that's still hellbent on domesticating our natural wildness*. Although awareness is slowly improving, we're still enmeshed in a society geared to convince us that a women's value lies in her looks, (pretty/young/sexy) and how nice she is. (compliant/quiet/sacrificing) Our authentic feminine nature is in truth something *deeply fiercer.*

Women are born with abundant strength and courage, traits our mostly male-dominated culture would still rather not have us express. The cultural norm is still to treat women as the "weaker sex," … just ask my granddaughter, who says the girls coach goes easy on the female athletes while boys of the same age are already heavily drilled in athletic skills. Of course we end up weaker when we're not given the opportunity to develop our strength from a young age! Still, all women have access to their authentic fierce nature, the very nature that's our best guide on the road.

Like many women, one of the reasons I became a nomad was a yearning for freedom. Long before becoming a nomad, I craved more meaning in my life, and felt out of place following a conventional life path. Freedom for me has always been about embracing life experiences that have challenged me to question my role in society, and I'm no stranger to reinventing myself. I've married and divorced twice, raised my kids as a single Mom, got involved in a Christian cult, then was born again (again), and then pagan. I was a sexual swinger in my 40's with my second husband, who turned out to be a full-blown covert narcissist. (Boy did I miss...ahem...ignore...those warning signs!) I lost close to 100 pounds to become sexually attractive, a story I'll tell in Chapter three. I was also a perfectionist, caretaker, co-dependent ... and dealing with debilitating bouts of depression, anxiety, and shame. To top it all off, in 2005 I developed disabling symptoms of an autoimmune disorder, taking me on another journey altogether.

Now that I'm on the road, I feel freer and happier than ever - as an earth-loving-spiritual-lesbian-vandwelling nomad. In a backward kind of way, the experiences of my past helped me get closer to my most authentic self, by showing me *who I'm NOT.*

As I explored different identities, I came to realize they defined *who I thought I should be ...not who I really was.* Because of the rejection and trauma caused by my father, I craved external validation, which eventually became unbearably painful. When I reached the point in my life when it felt like my soul was invisible, I came to understand that I could no longer tolerate a life that felt unbearable, just to be nice, safe, or approved of.

I've always felt most aligned with my authentic self when I'm close to nature…and living now as a van-dwelling nomad *I've never felt more comfortable in my own skin.*

Women Are Natural Nomads.

Many Women on the road have had childhood experiences camping or traveling, and my own experience included an annual summer family camping trip on a pristine Adirondack lake. It was there I learned primitive camping skills while tent camping in the primal forest, perfectly content without running water or electricity. It was there I connected to the peace and healing power of nature, and spent many happy childhood hours exploring the shoreline, hiking the forest, or floating blissfully in a canoe under a black-velvet sky shimmering with stars.

Looking back, I can remember my child-self staring out of windows longing to see more of the world. Then, like most adult women, I spent many years working and caretaking … first my children and then my aging parents. As a single Mom, I was employed for 20 years as a Patient Care Advocate with Planned Parenthood, working a second job cleaning houses and businesses. In 2010, after the kids were grown and my parents had passed, I fulfilled my dream of becoming a Certified Martha Beck Life Coach and established a women's only Life Coaching business, Pure Light coaching.com. (Now closed, but once a life coach always a life coach!)

Life has a way of interrupting the best-laid plans, and during that year, the disabling symptoms of muscle and brain dysfunction that I'd been living with since 2005 began to worsen. By 2012 I was permanently disabled, unable to drive and mostly homebound. I wasn't a quitter, but sadly resigned myself to making the best of the life I'd been dealt.

Before the illness, I was busy and active … steadily employed, raising my kids, taking care of my parents, establishing my life coaching business, hiking, working out, bike riding, socializing … then the onset of chronic illness left me isolated and alone. I'd lost my identity as a contributing member of the workforce, and while my two grown daughters were now immersed in working and raising their families, I'd lost much of my ability to participate normally in family and social events. My professional and personal life came to a screeching halt, and with my sole income of Social Security Disability, I struggled just to pay rent, fought constantly with the utility company to have lights and heat, and barely stayed afloat financially from month to month. I felt useless and left behind.

I tried to stay positive, but the struggle with my body often caused despair. In 2014, after a debilitating loss of muscle function and a trip to the emergency room, I began to feel suicidal. I literally dragged myself to a counselor to deal with severe depression. It took so much out of me just to get to the office I would sit on her couch wrapped in a blanket and struggle not to pass out. I couldn't imagine living my life with such limited functioning, and hopelessness threatened to take me down.

Thankfully, counseling with a compassionate and skillful therapist got me over the worst of the depression, and in 2015 the symptoms inexplicably began improving. I gained some mobility and was granted an unexpected reprieve from the severest symptoms of fatigue, pain, and muscle dysfunction. My body cooperated in sitting up for more than a few hours at a time, and I had fewer "crashes," - bouts when I couldn't function at all. Socializing was now possible with careful pacing, and I could walk more than a few feet without my muscles failing. I started driving again and was *ECSTATIC* to regain some of my lost independence.

I yearned more than ever to really LIVE my life, and not just exist.

I'd been granted a second chance!

In 2015, after coming home from my family's annual camping trip to the Adirondacks, I wrote in my journal, "If I could live this way, I'd be healed." My soul was calling me to a new life. What before had been a curiosity about nomadic life now became an obsession. I researched RVs, watched countless hours of YouTube videos on nomadism, and dreamt about living on the road close to the healing energy of Mother Earth.

As a Martha Beck trained Life Coach, I'd learned about **Wildly Improbable Goals ...W.I.G.s for short.** W.I.G.s are the dreams so far removed from our current reality we can't see a clear path to them, the dreams and desires that feel so far out of reach they seem unrealistic. W.I.G.s are

21

the sacred desires leading us to our most authentic life, and my W.I.G. was to become a nomad … ***and I had no idea how to make it happen!***

The dream wouldn't let me go. There were days I would feel pure exhilaration thinking I could do it, followed by weeks or months plunged into feeling scared sh*tless. I even talked myself out of it for a while.

It was the first time in my life I'd considered a major move that was intentionally positive, instead of the past relocating that was driven more by financial necessity than desire. By 2016 the pull was so strong I couldn't resist it, and I began actively planning. I penned budgets and timelines and started vehicle hunting, finally narrowing my choice down to some kind of van. With very little credit or disposable income, I consciously held the faith that an affordable vehicle would appear.

The day I saw the Big Green Uplander mini-van, I knew that was it!

The mini-van would be an easy vehicle to drive, convert and maintain, and just the right size for me to handle. The night before I bought the van I was wide awake with insomnia, anxiously laboring over lists of pros and cons. Still unsure of what the hell I was doing, my scared brain was going nuts trying to talk me out of it, but by the end of the next day, with a family member co-signing, I had my wheels!

Now sh*t was getting REAL! I made firm plans to move out of the apartment where I'd lived alone for 8 years and to move in with my oldest daughter for a few months while I saved for the van build.

By March of 2017, I'd moved and put the last of my stuff in storage. (Which I later ended up getting rid of!) My son-in-law helped me do a simple van build with a bed and shelving, and in June of 2017, I launched!

Staying near what was then my home base, I spent the summer exploring the Central Adirondacks in NY state, moving up and down the Route 30 corridor, boondocking at free campsites and a few paid campgrounds. (Boondocking: Camping or living in your vehicle without hooking up to water, electricity or waste receptacles, usually in free areas.) This was my test flight ... I'd given up my own place and purged most of my belongings to follow this irresistible dream. I had no idea if I'd be able to pull it off, or love it as much as I'd imagined. My routine in the beginning was *raw*. I was exhausted, anxious, often in pain - and the summer was exceptionally wet, rainy and buggy in the Adirondacks. ***Despite the struggle, the victorious feeling of finally DOING IT outweighed all the discomforts***!

As the summer wound down, I knew I would have to head out of the wintry Northeast to warmer climates if I wanted to continue vandwelling, and the Southwest pulled me like a magnet.

I discovered the snowbird destination of Quartzsite, Arizona and by October of 2017 found myself traveling solo across the country, boondocking in Walmarts, Cracker Barrels and Pilot Truck Stops, from NY state all the way across the continent to Arizona. I'd never driven that far in my life … much less alone, sleeping in a van! It took me ten days, and when I finally reached Arizona, it felt like I'd just accomplished one of the biggest W.I.G.S of my life! My first stop in Arizona was "standing on the corner of Winslow, Arizona," a corny thrill I'd looked forward to since the beginning of my journey!

Of course, it wasn't all perfect … there were times of absolute misery on the road … but I have absolutely ZERO REGRETS. Chronic illness still affects my journey, but I'm doing it! Creating my nomadic journey has been one of the greatest challenges of my life, taking guts and maybe a pinch of crazy … but the confidence, peace, and community I've found are priceless. I've seen vistas of soul-moving beauty and traveled places I would've never seen just sitting around in my old apartment. I've been delighted to meet astounding varieties of humans, and after living happily single for many years, even met my life partner Nancy on the desert when she walked by my camping spot under the cactus every day!

Even when I'm struggling, I feel ALIVE. I'm out there experiencing the world. I am FREE!

Remembering my "Why," is crucial in keeping me going … following my deep cravings to see more of the world, expanding my view, living in nature and having *personal freedom defined only by myself.*

Your Inner Wild Woman knows your own personal WHY.

Your WHY doesn't have to be grand or elaborate, but it does have to be personally meaningful to have the emotional force to keep you going.

Do you know your WHY, your purpose, what's driving you? (No pun intended!) Getting clear on your WHY keeps you connected to the *emotional energy of your dreams* - and gives you the motivation to keep moving towards their eventual fulfillment.

> *"If you have yet to be called an incorrigible, defiant woman, don't worry, there is still time."*
> ~ *Clarissa Pinkola Estés*

Each chapter is followed by prompts to help you DIG DEEPER. The following practices will help get you clear on your WHY. The Companion Journal To Wild Women On the Road, found on Amazon, contains the same exercises for each chapter.

DIG DEEPER: DISCOVER YOUR COMPELLING WHY

"I write because I don't know what I think until I read what I say." - Flannery O'Conner, female author and novelist

One of the most effective tools to help you clarify your WHY is journaling.

Journaling is therapeutic, creative, magic. Getting your thoughts, feelings, and daydreams down on paper slows your brain down long enough to gain clarity, allowing your creative mind to form new connections and insights.

Whenever I've journaled, the path to my dreams has often appeared. This isn't about magical thinking … but rather about doing the work of putting intentions down in writing. *This is your commitment to saying yes.* Saying YES to our dreams sharpens our vision to be alert to possibilities, and invites opportunities that we might not have considered.

EXERCISES

HOW TO KEEP A JOURNAL. Get a notebook, or some other way to collect your thoughts. Then, forget about fancy spelling, penmanship or grammar. Your journal is only for you, unless you're sharing your deepest self with someone highly trustworthy. Stash it somewhere where your private thoughts will stay private.

TIPS for journaling:

If you've never journaled before: Find a quiet space, grab your pen, put pen to paper, and write the FIRST THING that comes into your mind, even if it's a grocery list. Date each journal entry.

Listen internally to what comes up, and write just one sentence about that. Then another. You got it …the trick is to just start writing.

Don't censor. Everyone has their own journaling style. For some it's a diary of events, for others, a stream of consciousness of memories and emotions.

Because it's such an effective tool, I've encouraged every client I've coached to journal. Give it a try.

Start by journaling all the reasons WHY you want to become a nomad.

JOURNAL PROMPTS

1. Write down your W.I.G. (Wildly Improbable Goal.)

Example W.I.G: "I dream of traveling the Southwest full-time in a mini-van!"
Don't be afraid to make it *BIG, UNREALISTIC, AND IMPOSSIBLE!* That's the whole point of a W.I.G.!

Tips for your W.I.G: Don't censor! Write it all down even if sounds crazy!

Keep your emotional state light and carefree as you describe your W.I.G.

Grasping at what you want can squeeze the energy out of your dreams, so… ONCE YOU WRITE DOWN YOUR W.I.G., LET IT GO.

Trust that the Universe will provide the way. I promise you, this type of faith can manifest miracles.

2. Find Your Why.

Review the list below of reasons to become a van dweller. Pick the ones that light you up, or add your own, then answer these questions to clarify your WHY:

Which ones gave you an emotional zing, and why?

What do you picture when you fantasize about your life on the road?

What are some important values that you think makes van life meaningful to you? Living close to Nature? Freedom? Authenticity?

Write as much as you can about what comes up to clarify your WHY.

Reasons to become a van dweller:
Freedom
Traveling
Live Close to Nature
Financial Hardship

To Save Money
To Escape an Unhappy Life
To be Done With a Conventional Materialistic Lifestyle
Health Reasons
To Have Control Over Your Life
To Escape/Hide From Someone or Something
To LIVE before you die
To Live Authentically
To Find a Like-Minded Community
To Heal
To Live a More Meaningful Life
To See More Of The World

3. Write about childhood or past experiences that you think may have inspired your dreams of a nomadic lifestyle. (Camping. Traveling. Experiencing other cultures.)

What are some specific skills you've learned from those experiences? (Adaptability to living without conveniences. Familiarity with outdoor living. Ability to step out of your comfort zone.)

4. When you journal, describe your *feelings* about becoming a nomad. Include your fears, hopes, imagination, plans … and *start a regular practice journaling these thoughts and feelings.* Keeping a journal is a fascinating way to see where we were and how far we've come!

Some women burn their journals after a time. Some save them to look back on. If you've journaled about an especially painful experience, releasing the past by burning it up in a fire can be a beautifully therapeutic ritual.

"Expressive writing is a route to healing — emotionally, physically, and psychologically.
~ Dr. James Pennebaker, author of Writing to Heal.

CHAPTER TWO: FEAR; OUR BIGGEST OBSTACLE

"Fearlessness is like a muscle. I know from my own life the more I exercise it the more natural it becomes to not let my fears run me" – Arianna Huffington

Driving the first 15 minutes of my solo road trip from New York state to Arizona, I got lost. Somehow, I'd gotten on the highway *headed in the wrong direction.* I couldn't believe it. This was how the biggest trip of my life was going to start out?

On the second day, I was treated to a full blown panic attack on the Pennsylvania Turnpike. With my body trembling and tears streaming down my face, I kept it together long enough to get off the highway and find a place to recover. It ended my trip for the day, and forced me to find overnight parking in an area not on my carefully planned route.

Somewhere around Illinois, a big crawly Brown Recluse spider appeared on the inside of my windshield and started creeping towards me …while I was driving SMACK IN THE MIDDLE OF ROUTE 40 WITH NOWHERE TO SAFELY PULL OVER.

In Oklahoma City, after driving past dark to avoid a line of severe thunderstorms, I found a Walmart, and after asking permission to park overnight, settled in. At midnight I got the first unfriendly knock of my nomadic journey … a grumpy security guard kicked me out of the Walmart parking lot, in spite of having prior permission.

Alone in a strange city, alone, I had no idea where to go.

I've been approached by intimidating panhandlers, and once had a really creepy guy come into camp and ask me outright if I was camping alone. Since the start I've had many fearful encounters, one of them I've written about on my website cosmicnomadvoyager.com/my-scariest-nomad-experience/. Parked in a dark forest and unable to reach my partner parked up the hill, a group of drunk hooligans, all men, pulled into the campsite next to me. The light of fire flickered on their faces as they hooted and hollered about women's p*ssies. The experience I write about there still ranks as #1 scariest!

Obviously, I'm no stranger to fear! It's a wonder I didn't turn around and quit. Living on the road is no joke! But I've survived ONE HUNDRED PERCENT of the scary experiences, and they didn't stop me from living a life I love. I've learned that I'm capable of successfully handling each situation I encounter, despite the fear!

What do you feel after reading about my experiences? Are chills running up and down your spine? Is your heart speeding up a bit? Are you saying to yourself, *"Oh Hell NO, that's not for me!"*

That, my love, is your FEAR BRAIN telling you that your dreams are not safe.

What's interesting is this - what you're feeling is being triggered by events happening *only in your imagination! I hope I haven't discouraged you from your nomad dreams...I'm living a life that I absolutely love ... but as you can see there are very real physical, emotional and mental effects of FEAR.*

Fear can be a potent adversary to living the life of our dreams.

The way fear shows up for women is different than men, and has a significant impact on our decisions and experiences. We've internalized fears that we aren't physically safe *because of our gender*, for very good reasons. We can solve any problem, but women have different physical capabilities that for the most part men don't have to figure into their experience on the road.

That being said, if we mindfully examine the probability of the things we fear most, chances are they will NEVER happen. And when the unexpected does come up, we learn we have more than adequate coping skills, some we never knew we had.

When planning our life on the road, practical matters often get the blame for holding us back, like how to purge our stuff, get our finances straight, or purchase a vehicle ... which are all valid. But if we look closer, we may find ***our obstacles may be more internal than external.***

Understandably so.

Fear, and its impact on our mind and body, starts in the brain, arising from an ancient brain structure called the amygdala. The *"fight or flight"* response originates here, and in more primitive times it kept us alive when we were being stalked by large toothy predators. Among other things, this automatic response makes our heart race, quickens our breathing, contracts our muscles, and signals our adrenal glands to release adrenalin and cortisol - the "get the heck out of here" hormones that jack up our systems so we can avoid becoming a human Tiger snack.

Sometimes instead of fight or flight, the perceived threat triggers a "freeze" response. This came in handy in keeping us alive hiding in the primal forest, but if being frozen in fear keep us from moving forward towards our dreams, we get stuck.

Here's the tricky thing ... the fear response of our brain is only geared towards survival - it responds without any rational thought. *It can't distinguish between a real threat and a perceived threat happening only in our imagination.*

The fear part of our brain has also been called the LIZARD BRAIN ... and has only one job - to keep us safe.

That same fear response in the "lizard brain" that tells us to run from the Tiger is precisely the same response that tells us to avoid at all costs all the worst things that could ever happen ... even when they're only in our imagination!

Worse, when we can't stop worrying, the fear response gets stuck in the ON position, resulting in chronic stress that clouds our thinking, interferes with creative problem-solving, and keeps us from clearly hearing our innate wisdom.

So, you can predict what will happen when we start dreaming about leaving behind our nice warm house and familiar routines for the uncertainty of nomadic life! Our fear brain just about loses it … screaming in our head, *"DEAR GOD WE WON'T BE SAFE, WE HAVE TO STAY LOCKED UP SAFELY INSIDE AND WHAT ARE YOU THINKING YOU ARE GOING TO DIE!!!"*

To Our Primitive Fear Brain, Change Equals Threat.

Radical change feels life-threatening, with good reason. The fear brain, combined with our socialized self, gives us a sense of "ego" …. of who we are and where we belong in the world. Identifying with this *ego-self* has kept us safe, warm, fed, and hopefully, loved. Subconsciously, the ego is tied to our very survival. To a small helpless child, losing the support of caretakers and social groups is *literally life-threatening*, so to feel safe we are biologically set up to agree to cultural conditioning, starting in infancy. This is an advantageous psychological mechanism for the perpetuation of the species, but not so great when the boundaries that once kept you safe are now preventing you from fulfilling your dreams.

We end up with a *social self*, the safe self we present to the world, and an *essential self*…the authentic self we're born with that craves the deepest desires of our souls.

The ego, run by the social self, will show us any number of horror stories to keep us in the safe status quo:

"You'll be destitute. You'll get assaulted. You'll be alone. You'll lose it all. You're crazy. You'll die of loneliness … or starvation … or lost alone in the wilderness!"

We'll even find evidence that all of this is true.

If we want to fulfill our dreams, we must use our thinking brain to consciously question the motives of the social self. To give in to its fear and its overwhelming imperative to feel safe, is to never live the life of our dreams.

That doesn't mean we never feel fear. I've been terrified at times… even before getting on the road. There were times I believed my fear. Here I was planning on leaving a warm, comfortable, predictable life to go out alone and unsheltered into the world … living in nothing but a small vehicle with no modern conveniences and *WHY THE HELL WOULD I WANT TO DO THAT????*

*My fear brain w*as trying to discourage me from making such a drastic change. I wanted reassurance that my decision to live on the road was the right one, but there was no crystal ball to predict my future. When it came right down to it, I had to leap into the life I desired, in spite of my fears. This quote from Terence McKenna says it all:

"Nature loves courage. You make the commitment and nature will respond to that commitment by removing impossible obstacles. This is the trick. This is what all these teachers and philosophers who really counted, who

really touched the alchemical gold, this is what they understood. This is the shamanic dance in the waterfall. This is how magic is done. By hurling yourself into the abyss and discovering it's a feather bed."

When all is said and done, all you can do is leap.

Refusal To Give In To Fear Is Called Courage.

By telling myself better stories about my future, I calmed my fearful lizard brain.

While it was possible something could happen to me on the road, I knew by looking at my past that I'd been able to handle EVERY SINGLE PROBLEM I'D EVER ENCOUNTERED IN MY LIFE. This was evidence I could deal with just about anything life had to throw at me. If you're like most women, you've already successfully dealt with your share of difficult and stressful situations.

So what about the situations that DON'T turn out fine? Looking at all the frightening things happening in the world, *don't we have real reasons to be afraid?* If you're brave enough, go ahead and google this: *yearly deaths from household accidents.* The truth is that even tucked away inside four walls, we are never truly safe!

Women have a different set of fears to confront than men, and those factors color the experience of a woman's nomadic life. That's not to say one gender has it better than another, just that we have different issues to face.

One of women's biggest fears on the road is the risk of assault, and I had an acute awareness of this myself. The truth for women is that it could happen anywhere, anytime, even in traditional housing, but *get this - the risk is statistically much lower on the road.*

To put it into perspective, check out these facts in the article, "Sleeping Alone In The Woods While Female:"

"The National Park Service reported 83 rapes *(one in 3,527,951 visitors)* on its public lands in 2014, compared with 84,041 reported rapes (one in 3,794 people) in the rest of the country.

This translates to a .000028% chance of being assaulted on public lands.

From the article: "When people say a woman choosing to venture alone in the wilderness is reckless, it's very possibly due to a lack of understanding about the realities of sexual assault. *Women are most likely to be assaulted in their own homes or in a private space*, according to Jennifer Wesely, who studies violence against women at the University of North Florida. Fear of strangers seems like a misconception, too, considering that more than three-quarters of women who are sexually assaulted know their attackers."

While it doesn't take into account the probability of unreported assaults, in a 2014 report, the Bureau of Land Management, which oversees hundreds of thousands of miles of free national land in the West, where thousands of female nomads flock every year, **reported ZERO rapes.**

Security is an illusion, whether we're in a van or million-dollar mansion.

That's not to say a dangerous situation will never come up, but common sense, awareness, and confidence go a long way in ensuring our safety on the road. *Later in this chapter I'll go into detailed instructions on how to develop your confidence.*

Women also face underlying emotional fears when considering a nomadic life. As women, we're taught to minimize our own needs and repress our own desires, or more accurately, we're shamed for having dreams that don't revolve around everyone else.

For women whose self-care has been at the bottom of their priority list for years, it can be emotionally challenging to make a decision based solely on their own wants and needs. To become a nomad, we must leave behind familiar and comfortable roles as women, and for most of us, it means exploring completely unknown emotional territory. Leaving my grown daughters and grandkids to travel across the country was one of the hardest things I've ever done. It felt selfish, brought up grief and other painful emotions, forcing me to re-evaluate our relationships and how things would change being a long-distance Mom and Grandma.

Many of us start out our nomad life confused. My heart was broken leaving my family to follow my dreams, but it also forced me to recognize how emotionally dependent I'd become on them over the years. I'd lived practically in the same neighborhood for most of their lives…and on my way out to Arizona, the separation felt so intense I was tempted to turn around. Thankfully I didn't.

Now we've settled into a beautiful routine that continues to keep our family close. I spend most of my time in the Fall and Winter in the warm climate of the Southwest, and when Spring weather warms up, travel back to the Northeast to spend time with my family.

It takes courage to face the emotional pain of change, but more painful than change is regret. As the French-American erotica novelist Anais Nin said, *"And the day came when the risk to remain tight in a bud was more painful than the risk it took to blossom."*

Eventually, my nomadic journey became an opportunity for me to *discover who I am … NOT defined by family roles.* The sharp grief I felt leaving my family slowly resolved, and now my daughters and grandkids have an example of a strong woman living her deepest desires, in spite of her fears.

Can We Do It Alone?

As far as women being the "weaker sex," working for Planned Parenthood and serving women for over 20 years, and then becoming a Life Coach for women, gave me a unique view of women's fierceness.

Women are POWERFUL. We bleed for seven days every month … going on with business as usual while dealing emotionally, financially, and physically with this intense process. We can grow human beings inside our bodies, then labor intensely to bring them into the world. *We endure, we survive, we recover, we thrive, in a society that is still trying to break our spirit.* Every woman alive has inner emotional and mental strength … while at the same time, being effectively *conditioned by society to deny their inner toughness.* I can't tell you the number of women I've met over the years surviving in soul-crushing conditions, who offhandedly dismiss their strength.

Realizing the truth of who we are as women is our path to empowerment and to living the life we crave!

Facing the Fear of Loneliness

When we finally decide to purge our belongings, give up modern conveniences, and take off to live on the road, it often upsets the status quo in our family and social circles. Loss of support can be a real issue when we've chosen to follow the path less traveled, and we may have to face a two-fold fear of not just loneliness, but of being alone. When I left the East Coast, I left behind my entire support system. Thankfully, within a few months of being out West, I'd gained a new network of supportive women!

Fear of being alone is an issue many solo women van-dwellers must face. No wonder – the trait to be a social creature is probably coded into our very DNA. Some of the fear we experience is biological - in our not so far off past *women's dependency on men was a biological necessity.*

The biological imperative for women to reproduce kept them in a vulnerable position, with few exceptions. While men left the family circle for days at a time to provide - to hunt, or in modern times to work, women stayed close to the hearth, tied to the cycles of reproduction. I'm not a sociologist, but it's not a stretch to see that our vulnerability ended up as permission to define us as the weaker sex. We became second-class citizens, with little or no rights to our own bodies and voices.

We're socialized from a young age to accept the standard gender roles for women, even in these modern times. While there is a movement for change, we can see gender roles still prevalent in preteen and teen entertainment, and as adults, we're bombarded by a constant stream of media that establishes the social code for our looks, behavior, and sexuality. Girls are still socialized from childhood to learn that a women's role is to care-take physically, emotionally, mentally, get along and be nice - while the masculine role is to be strong, brave, and protective. In reality, the essential nature of each gender defies these standardized roles.

While we could debate that most women don't have the muscle mass of men, our exceptional emotional strength and problem-solving capabilities more than balance out our lesser physical ability. We have a high tolerance for pain, (think about women in labor) along with a gritty persistence and emotional intelligence that benefits us out on the road.

Women are natural problem solvers. While men rule the world, women keep it running smoothly behind the scenes. We have an innate intelligence that allows us to perform the balancing act of mental labor that keeps the wheels turning. An interesting study commissioned by Bright Horizons reports in the 2017 Family Index that "women are still lifting far more of their share of the mental load than men." (https://www.brighthorizons.com/about-us/press-releases/mental-load-impact-working-mothers-study) And at the time of this book's updated version, that marker still hasn't changed much.

I have hope that things are changing for us, but at age 77 Gloria Steinem said this about gender equality: "I'm old, but the movement is young. Every social justice movement has to last at least 100 years or it doesn't really get absorbed into society. We're only 30 or 40 years into this!"

Even ancient mythology shows us impressive examples of the fierce nature of women. While the Western view of the sacred feminine has been diluted to a motherly, soft, and nurturing figure, ancient feminine archetypes revealed a more complex picture. Female archetypes were portrayed as competent hunters, (Diana) or incredibly powerful figures that mercilessly destroyed their foes. (Kali) The sacred feminine was depicted as ferocious, empowered and capable. This natural fierceness of women has been socially discouraged and repressed in modern times - but it's indeed *who we are*. If we reflect on it, each one of us can recall times in our lives when we've found the inner strength and determination to get difficult things done.

Women are still being socialized differently than men when it comes to dealing with strong emotions like fear. Little girls are socialized to be nice, to look and feel helpless, repressing "noisy" emotions of indignation or anger. Little boys are socialized to suck it up and be brave. Both genders ultimately suffer from this socialization.

So How Do We Deal With Fear?

Each one of those frightening situations I told you about eventually turned out fine. All I can say is *I must be a stubborn goddess-bitch of a woman ... I refused to give up!*

After getting lost, I turned around and got back on the highway, this time driving in the right direction. After the panic attack, I found a welcoming Walmart parking lot to recover. In Oklahoma, after getting booted out of the Walmart parking lot at 12AM, I quickly found another spot to stealth camp for the night.

As for that spider, it was a case of him or me ... and I wasn't surrendering. I beat it up with a rolled-up map and pulled off at the next exit to make sure my beating did the job.

In every single circumstance I'd been presented with, I was able to find my courage, and found I was equipped with the feminine superpower of problem-solving that every woman has been gifted.

With the panhandler and the creepy guy, I channeled my inner warrior Goddess energy.

The panhandler surprised me at my van window, while I was sitting in my driver's seat at a truck stop with my head down in my phone. While there are times I'm moved to share with panhandlers, this wasn't one of them. When I looked up and saw him, I put my hand up in a firm "STOP" gesture and shook my head no. His expression implied that he didn't want to take no for an answer, and when he lingered a moment too long outside of my window, *I didn't act "nice," and I didn't smile.* I held eye contact, and focused on the energy of "GET THE F*CK AWAY FROM ME" in my body. He walked away.

I'd made a mistake and let my guard down. Instead of being aware of my surroundings, my head was in my phone. I was unaware of him until he was right at my window! Lesson learned!

The creepy guy incident happened when I was solo van camping in the Adirondacks. Camped near a historical trout stream, it wasn't unusual to see fishermen walking through the area. I was parked within a few feet of a well-trafficked road, and with the Adirondacks being one of the safest areas to camp, felt comfortable there.

One morning an RV pulled in across the road from me, driven by a lone fisherman. He came through my camp decked up in full-on fishing gear and a mosquito net entirely obscuring his face. Unlike the other fishermen, he didn't respect the boundaries of my campsite and walked right through it. The next day he started up a conversation … asking directly if I was camping alone. I lied, telling him no. He chatted for a few minutes and then went off to fish. Coming back through the campsite later that day, **he walked into camp behind me without warning,** *scaring the sh*t out of me.* Thankfully he continued on without incident. The next day I psyched myself up to confront him, and seeing him pull up, I sat on the bumper of my car in full view of the road, with my knife, wasp spray and walking stick close at hand. **I CONSCIOUSLY FOCUSED ON FEELING STRONG CONFIDENT ENERGY IN MY BODY.**

You know it, I was terrified! My heart was pounding, but I refused to be intimidated.

As he approached, I said, "I want to talk to you," in a strong, confident voice. I stood up straight and held eye contact with him. In a calm but assertive tone, I communicated how inappropriate it was for him to ask if I was camping alone, and that sneaking up behind me was terrible etiquette at the least. He was very apologetic, and admitted he knew right away that I was camping alone - even though I'd placed the "big man sneakers" outside of my (empty) tent to make it look like I had a male companion! (I threw them away after that.) I don't know how much my knife, wasp spray and walking stick would have helped me, but they gave me *the feeling of confidence.*

After talking to him, my gut told me he was just socially awkward, lonely, and probably harmless. He acted appropriately after that and left me alone. I stayed at the campsite, but *still, never let down my guard.*

I've also made newbie mistakes that in hindsight were potentially dangerous. When I was camping in the Coconino forest in Arizona, an obviously disadvantaged couple walked by my van every day. One morning the woman started yelling outside my window when I was

46

inside the van - and I opened the door and poked my head out. She wanted to know what time it was. With my attention on her, her partner could have snuck up behind me, a potentially dangerous situation. They asked for rides even after repeatedly telling them no. In that same area, a raging drunk was dropped off across the road from me with nothing more than a tent, which he was unable to assemble in his highly inebriated state. These were people that definitely set off warning bells … a tightening in my gut that alerted me to pay attention … but as a newbie I was reluctant to make the effort to leave and find another spot. I was probably OK, but looking back I cringe - the risk for trouble definitely outweighed the inconvenience of having to move. I was lucky.

Since then I've had other potentially dangerous encounters on the road. You can read more about them on my website, cosmicnomadvoyager.com. My best defense in these situations has been my attitude of "take no sh*t."

Talking to other female van dwellers, it seems we all have varying degrees of caution. I've met women so over the top paranoid and steeped in fear that they rarely venture outside their vans, and others that don't seem to have any caution at all. Personally, it doesn't make any sense for me to be on the road if I'm too scared to relax and enjoy the healing beauty of nature just outside of my van.

Confidence Is An Antidote To Fear.

My philosophy is that confidence is our first line of defense, even if we fake it in the beginning. Experienced women nomads agree that while there are practical things

47

we can do to protect ourselves, ***most of a women's safety*** is psychological. Predators don't want to deal with strength and confidence, they're looking for the weakest prey.

When you're dealing with a boundary-violating *cad*, (Cad is an old word describing a man who treats women badly.) use this handy acronym, C.A.D., to remember the attitude you want to project:

Confident.
Assertive.
Direct.

Look **C**onfident by making your posture straight and firm. Be **A**ssertive (not aggressive), by stating clearly in a commanding tone of voice, what you expect. Be **D**irect with your words and eye contact.

C.A.D. sounds like this:

"Please stop walking through my campsite."
"I don't want company."
"Please leave."
"I'm calling the police."
"No."

Awareness is crucial. Pay attention to your surroundings. Don't engage in a conversation with a stranger just to be nice. Notice who your neighbors are. Don't ignore gut feelings. Park your vehicle facing out for a quick exit and always put your keys in the same place for easy access. Always lock yourself in at night. Don't leave valuables easily visible, stash them or cover them up if you leave your vehicle. If you have a self-defense weapon, make sure you are confident in using it. Talk to other women vandwellers and nomads, develop your own routine for safety and stick to it. Don't hesitate to get in your van and drive away, even if it's inconvenient!

Camping out in the desert I met a solo woman who seemed to be a magnet for attracting unwanted attention from "friendly" men. She didn't want to appear rude, and was afraid that if she didn't act "nice" they'd give her a hard time. Unfortunately my experience has been that she was right, some men will get angry when you're not friendly to them, but it was a terrible defense ... *her niceness just encouraged even more aggressive behavior!* She spent much of her time in fear, trying to figure out what to say to these guys, which only seemed to attract even more trouble to her. By then I was no longer solo camping, and my partner and I coached her repeatedly on how to be assertive and direct. She was in constant worry over her safety, and it was heartrending to see a woman struggling with so much fear.

While being cautious and prepared is a good investment in our safety, constant worry is a waste of our precious life energy. It deprives us of good feelings and experiences available in the present moment.

How do we want to live? Are we living life right now, or are we spending our precious time immersed in some imaginary adverse event that is only happening in our minds? For a female nomad, balancing safety with our enjoyment of the nomad journey is a valuable skill!

Life is a risk no matter what, and fear will steal our dreams if we let it.

We may not have control over whatever life has in store for us, but our *response* is something we can choose.

Live Your Dreams In Spite Of Fear!

I heard it said once that our deepest fear is that we'll abandon ourselves. What we're really terrified of is that at the moment we need it most, we won't have adequate strength or courage, and we'll let ourselves down. There might be something to that.

Our underlying fear isn't that we'll fail others, but that ultimately we'll fail ourselves. As a Wild Woman Nomad, we'll have the opportunity to face that fear, and discover depths of strength and wisdom we may have never otherwise known.

We can never completely predict what's coming next in life. We have a choice - live in fear of the terrible things that could happen, or choose to imagine the best possible outcome. Imaginary worries are never real in the present moment, why not imagine the best!

My personal belief is that the Universe is inherently good, that 99% of the time, in the present moment, nothing bad is happening to us. My own personal experience is that when I started a conscious practice of focusing on the best possible outcomes, positive events seemed to occur more frequently. Maybe I was just training myself to *notice* the positive, but it doesn't really matter to me. Call it the law of attraction, faith, or coincidence … for me, this life philosophy helps free me from fear.

Anytime we have a major decision to make … "should I stay or should I go" … "should I take this risk" … ***REMEMBER THAT FEAR IS A TERRIBLE ADVISOR.***

Fear is noisy. It fills our heads with frightening thoughts and distracts us from living in the present moment. It doesn't care about our dreams. It exists to maintain the status quo and keep us from danger … even when the danger exists only in the imaginary future.

Feeling fear doesn't mean you're going the wrong way or making the wrong decision. ***Fear is a different sensation than following your gut.***

Instead of following the path of fear, ***go after what pulls you like a magnet.*** Stay with the magic of what lights you up inside!

Focus on your dreams, instead of your fear. Your desire for something more is sacred. Your right to live the life of your dreams is your fundamental human right.

Tell your fear brain that you're OK, you've got this. Reassuring your fearful lizard brain will keep it calm.

Remember that courage is not the absence of fear. Courage is doing the thing you're intensely afraid of, in spite of the fear. It's taking the leap, even when it looks absolutely crazy!

"The path of the Thriver is courage." ~ Melanie Tonia Evans

The next Dig Deeper prompts will help you navigate your way out of fear.

DIG DEEPER: HOW TO GET OUT OF THE FEAR TRAP

"A happy life seeks the truth; an unhappy life seeks safety first." ~ Jane Broughton

Tools to Deal With Fear

1. Breathing. The opposite of the fear response is the "rest and restore" response, which allows us to relax. To get into this rest and restore response, we need to activate the parasympathetic nervous system, done by consciously practicing slow and relaxed breathing.

Along with promoting healing and proper digestion, this relaxation response allows us to think clearly, and to tap into the problem-solving area of our brain, called the prefrontal cortex. If we choose to, it also enables us to access our higher spiritual wisdom, or higher self.

When we're stressed or afraid, we unconsciously take fast, shallow breaths. If we can change that breathing pattern to deep, slow, abdominal breathing, we can convince the fearful lizard brain that all is well.

Simple Instructions For Calming Breaths.

Put your hand on your abdomen, and breathe out in a soft exhale.

Breathe in slowly and deeply through your nose for about 4 seconds, expanding your lower abdomen like a balloon against your hand, and imagine your lungs filling from the bottom up. Keep your shoulders still, then expand your abdomen, then chest, as you inhale and your lungs fill.

Hold the breath briefly, then slowly exhale from your mouth, pursing your lips like you're blowing out a candle, feeling your abdomen deflate.

Repeat at least 3 times for instant stress relief.

If you feel dizzy, stop and take normal breaths.

This breathing short-circuits the fearful stress response and gets you back into the "rest and digest" response.

2. Loving Kindness Meditation. If we're habitually ruminating about what can go wrong, we'll remain chronically revved up on fear. If we want to make decisions from our wiser self, and not our stressed self, we first need to calm our fear brain.

When you find yourself getting stressed and imagining the worst, close your eyes and say these words to yourself, out loud or in your mind, *"May you be safe. May you be well. May you live in joy and peace. All is well."*

It can also be an effective practice to preface the words with "I AM."

"I am Safe, I am Well, I live in Joy and peace."

This practice is based on a Tibetan loving-kindness meditation, and although it may feel silly at first, this soothing language is helpful in calming our fear brain.

We're wired as humans to respond positively to a kind voice ... even when it's our own.

In Martha Beck's book, Diana Herself, she recommends adding endearing words to the meditation, saying "sweet friend, my love," or other similar endearments. You can find more information about this powerful practice in Martha Beck's book, Diana Herself: An Allegory of Awakening.

Anytime you feel fearful or stressed, repeat this practice until you feel calmer.

The night before I bought my van, fear was running so high I was tempted to back out. I consciously practiced deep breathing, repeating the reassuring statements: "May you be safe. May you be well. May you live in joy and peace. All is well." Fear kept returning in waves, but I refused to give into it, and focused on calming my hysterical primitive fear brain. Each time I did the practice, I could feel calm internal guidance pulling me towards the life I now love!

3. Re-program your response to fear. When we do a lot of worrying we create neurological pathways in the brain that keep us in a fear loop, a type of *worry program*. Our thinking brain is capable of *over-riding this fear program and re-programing us to worry less.*

Take a moment to imagine what you fear the most about living a nomadic life. Is it not having four walls? Fear of assault? A mechanical breakdown? Fear of loneliness?

WARNING: If you suffer from PTSD don't visualize a worse case triggering event.

1. Form a clear picture in your mind of what you fear.
2. Allow yourself to feel the stress triggered by that image.
3. Using the previous exercises, slow your breathing and use the loving-kindness meditation. ***The goal here is to learn to reduce your fear response.***

*Continue to breathe deeply and visualize the problem solved. Imagine yourself safe, strong and confident, having the resources to handle whatever comes up. You don't need to know how that will happen; you just need to let yourself **be in the positive feelings of this good visualization.** Don't censor your good imagination ... your fear brain will be telling you, "This isn't realistic!" Remember, with either a good scenario or bad, it's all just imagination! You're just playing!*

Focus on how you'll FEEL with the problem solved. Refuse to picture yourself lacking anything. Let your brain and body feel the relief of knowing everything turns out ok.

Put this "fear antidote" into practice whenever you feel stressed or have doubts about your life on the road.

Be sure to journal about what comes up with this exercise. Sometimes we aren't afraid of what we think we're afraid of.

4. Build Your Confidence.

Before I got on the road, I did my homework and made sure I had items that would get me out of a jam. These items may be different for you, the key is to increase your feeling of safety and confidence on the road.

Here's my list:

Small saw.
Hatchet.
Basic tools.
Portable battery bank with jumper cables.
Extra jumper cables.
Fix a flat.
Good Sam's Roadside assistance.
Small pocketknives throughout the van.
Box cutter.
Lots of batteries and flashlights.
Smartphone with Map apps.
At one point I had these: Foghorn. Wasp Spray. Huge pair of men's sneakers. I've since gotten rid of these items.
Since the original list I've added a tire thumper. It's a wooden bat.
I'm planning on adding a taser wand soon.

Before my long road trip to Arizona, I had my son-in-law give me a refresher course on how to change a flat tire, how to use the portable compressor, and how to jumpstart my vehicle.

*All of these things help me feel **confident that I can handle myself.***

If you haven't already, make a list of safety items you'll need for the road. If concerns of a physical attack are making you anxious, take a self-defense course for women. Watch YouTube videos on safety and self-defense. Have discussions with other women about safety.

Most important of all, make a commitment to yourself that you won't let fear be a dream thief!

"We must become ignorant of all we've been taught, and be instead, bewildered.... forget safety. Live where you fear to live. Destroy your reputation. Be notorious. I have tried prudent planning long enough, from now on, I'll live mad." ~ Rumi

CHAPTER THREE: TRUSTING YOUR WILD NATURE TO GUIDE YOU

"You don't need to figure anything out. You don't need to see how it all fits together. All you need is to practice directing your attention to the life you want."
~ Cheri Huber

The morning before signing the final paperwork for my mini-van, I was wide awake at five - AM - anxiety - o'clock, flooded with worry. In those wee hours I worked and re-worked budgets, considered and reconsidered my options, and *freaked the F***out.*

Those were some really hairy moments. I'd finally found the perfect vehicle … THE ONE … but fear threatened to throw me off the path to my dreams. I even contemplated backing out on the whole thing!

I allowed my logical brain to continue the task of working my budget, keeping my breathing deep and steady, and repeating the loving-kindness meditation (covered in chapter two Dig Deeper exercises) until my lizard brain *chilled the F*** out.*

Now, if I could just trust myself, this wild-assed dream of being on the road was just within reach.

In moments of calm, the decision to move ahead and purchase that van felt clear and expansive in my body.

In the practical everyday world, my decision to buy this van with the intention of making it my home on wheels made absolutely NO SENSE, but this magical vehicle was a magnet, PULLING me to have it.

I absolutely refused to give in to fear, and the next day, after some financial wrangling and the help of my daughter and son-in-law, the forest green mini-van, aka The Green Beastie, became mine!

Following our dreams may feel crazy, but sometimes the crazy decision is the absolute right one for us, and the so-called sensible one, the wrong one. I felt in my heart, gut, and soul that I was going in the right direction in buying that van - *a clear go-ahead from my Body Compass.*

Body Compass ... ok, what the heck is THAT? The Body Compass, a name coined by Martha Beck and taught in her Life Coaching program, is our internal guidance system directing us to our personal truth. Our **Body Compass** is found in *sensations* and physical responses that are *felt within* ... and not in our logical mind. We can't "think" the Body Compass. Like a compass that always points North, the Body Compass leads us to our most authentic life ... if we know how to tune in.

The Body Compass is a bundle of sensations we *feel in our body* that says, "Yes! This is great!" or "No way, don't even go there!" We store within ourselves the non-verbal *YES or NO* our body communicates to us in every moment. We've all experienced this - gut feelings warning us something is off, or goosebumps when we resonate deeply with the truth. *We can up-level this process by learning to access our inner guidance with conscious intent.*

The body is a container of exquisite emotions and feelings that help us navigate our world, but the problem for modern women is that we've been taught to cut ourselves off from those truth-telling sensations.

We Learn, as Women, That Following The Wild Nature Of Our Body Is Dangerous.

We've been conditioned to ignore our internal wisdom, while at the same time be hyper-focused on external appearances, mostly to please the rest of the world. In modern culture, media portrayals of women, including porn, determine the beauty ideal we should be striving for - *impossibly perfect, symmetrical, sexy, and young*. Take a look at the covers of women's magazines the next time you're standing in a checkout line, and you'll see exactly what I mean. **Conversely**, the threat of rape that every woman must deal with informs us that our bodies are a dangerous sexual temptation … and yet sexual predators want us to believe that it's our responsibility to keep all of this under control! As women, we're taught to disassociate from the power and beauty of our natural bodies, resulting in the least, in a type of soul numbness, and at the most, in many cases, self-hatred of our natural womanly selves. *Yet, our incredible, sexual, beautiful wild bodies hold some of our most sacred wisdom.*

Unfortunately, when we're cut off from our bodies through stress or cultural conditioning, we're cut off from the internal wisdom that guides us to live as our most authentic selves.

For many years I was at war with my body. Being a "fat" woman most of my adult life, I began craving the attention I saw thin "sexy" women getting, and made it my life-goal to be sexually desirable. What I didn't understand was this craving was driven by unhealed wounds of childhood neglect and abuse. ***I had deep-rooted feelings of not being good enough.***

To "fix" my body I became its dictator. I began depriving it of good food, making dieting a lifestyle, and forcing it into compliance with countless hours of exercise at the gym. I lost 100 pounds and got "into shape," applied layers of makeup, plucked, shaved, and added a fake tan and blond streaks in my hair. Focusing solely on my looks ***dulled my connection to the most deeply authentic part of myself, and overshadowed the messages of truth my body regularly tried to convey.*** The spiritual practices I'd invested in for years, like meditation, Yoga, and Reiki, took a back seat to the "making-myself-beautiful-to-get-attention-project."

And the project was a success. After achieving my goal to be outwardly attractive, I threw myself into a series of toxic relationships with men. After those failed, I became a swinger. Thinking I was looking for sexual empowerment, (not a bad thing in itself) the swinger scene provided me with more than enough sexual attention, and eventually, I married another swinger. I finally felt attractive and desirable, but the painful intimacy issues and low self-worth that led me down that path remained unhealed.

As time went on, I began resenting the price of "sexiness," spending countless hours on beauty maintenance and hard-earned cash at the beauty counter. The people I'd chosen to surround myself with, including the covert narcissist I married, were incapable of seeing my authentic self. All of it made zero contribution to my well-being, and eventually became sheer torture to my soul.

There's nothing inherently wrong with beauty regimes or sexual empowerment, but ironically, rejecting my authentic self created situations that brought even more painful rejections.

During that time, I was also caring for my Mother as she slowly lost her life to Alzheimer's Disease, and when she finally succumbed at the young age of 76, it woke me up. It was a poignant lesson in how short our lives really are, and *her death forced me to re-evaluate my own life. I was shocked to realize that I'd never felt much joy, or experienced deep intimacy with anyone, including myself.* By then I was struggling with severe insomnia, anxiety, depression, and an autoimmune condition, all unmistakable messages from my body that it was time to seek healing.

Those experiences ended up being painful, yet essential lessons. I gave up swinging, which was the last straw for the marriage, but *I was finally FREE*. Although I'd had years of counseling in the past, I recommitted to personal growth, going even deeper into unconscious layers of childhood wounds that had driven my life choices. Eventually, I made peace with my body and treated it tenderly instead of forcing it into submission, practicing self-massage with soothing essential oils and sending positive messages to every part of my body. Listening within, I learned that my body was longing for comfort, self-acceptance, and rest!

That healing journey of self-acceptance ultimately led to my current life on the road, and now my hair is super short, I wear jeans and tees, zero makeup, and feel more alive and at peace than ever!

So How Do We Answer The Questions - Who Am I and What Do I Really Want?

Many women will find my experience familiar. Beginning in childhood, we receive distinct orders from parents and authority figures to ignore the truth of our own bodies. We're told: "Be quiet, be nice, don't complain, don't be selfish." *What we're really being admonished to do is, "Don't speak the truth, ignore your discomfort, and never put your own needs first."*

By the time we're out of childhood, the messages from our sensitive Body Compass have been silenced, leaving us unable to make decisions guided by our deepest wisdom. When we're out of touch with our own being, we spend precious time and life energy moving in the wrong direction, choosing the wrong partners, the wrong careers, the wrong life.

The great news is, we can turn our lives around and bypass the outdated orders to ignore our own truth.

Once I made the decision to spend my life energy on more personally meaningful investments, my authentic Self started to make herself known. I finally achieved my Reiki

Master level, something I'd put off for 10 years, and the same month my marriage ended, started ten months of Life Coach training with the Martha Beck Institute.

When I learned about my own Body Compass in Martha Beck's book Finding Your Own North Star, it was a complete game changer. I realized I hadn't lived authentically for most of my adult life.

I'd found freedom from the acute emotional pain of not living authentically, but unfortunately the stress I'd put my body through finally took its toll. In 2010 the autoimmune symptoms I'd been dealing with for years escalated into severe disability.

I became unable to drive and was housebound. Experimenting unsuccessfully with various medical and alternative treatments, looking for anything that would heal me, I finally gave up on "fixing myself." The illness was teaching me, once again, that fixing myself wasn't what my body needed. Funny thing, when I gave up on fixing myself, and was forced to start *CARING FOR MYSELF*, it was then that the most debilitating symptoms began to ease up. Although I was far from normal, the muscle weakness and dysfunction improved, and I was able to drive again. I was ecstatic!

I felt like I'd been given a second chance at life, and started contemplating nomadic life after a family camping trip to the Adirondacks in 2015. By June of 2017, I was on the road living my dream. The disability of an autoimmune condition still adds an extra challenge, but my body, mind, and soul continue to thrive living a nomadic life close to nature! *My body knew what it needed, and I've never once regretted following its wisdom.*

As the years went by living as a nomad, my body healed in incremental steps. I even wrote another book about how living close to nature healed me, found on Amazon. *(600 Days as a Nomad; How the Mystical Power of Nature Healed My Body, Mind, and Soul.)*

The Body Is A Genius!

One of the huge advantages of learning our own Body Compass is that it knows where we truly belong, *long before our intellectual mind has it figured out.* When we're confused, we can count on our body's internal guidance system to lead us to our personal truth. How many times have we heard, "I had a gut feeling," or, "I should have listened to that little inner voice!" Our innate internal wisdom is unfailing, but how often do we second guess those quiet messages!

When it comes to making decisions, the rational, thinking conscious mind actually lags behind the intuition held in our body.

In his book, Incognito: The Secret Lives of the Brain, David Eagleman shares convincing research to support this. He describes what we're calling the Body Compass as a superior decision-making tool.

In the study, discussed by Eagleman, subjects picked cards from four decks, with each card representing a gain or loss of money. Two decks were stacked in their favor, while the other two were stacked to promote a loss. Subjects drew cards one at a time, and were asked at various points in the experiment to identify which decks were "good" and which were "bad."

The subject's autonomic nervous system, the unconscious system that regulates automatic responses including fight or flight, was closely monitored with each draw. By the 13th card, the measurements of the subject's responses showed they were having an unconscious reaction when they drew from a "bad" deck. *They already knew on a SUBCONSCIOUS level which decks were advantageous and which were not, but it took 12 more draws, up to 25 total, before the subjects CONSCIOUSLY knew which decks were favorable or unfavorable!* Eagleman related that "conscious knowledge of a situation was not required for making advantageous decisions."

Messages From Your Body Compass Can Reliably Guide Your Life!

If you're feeling the pull to jump into this radical life, it may be that your Body Compass is guiding you in that direction! When we're empowered from within our own bodies, we're able to live fully in our individual freedom, happiness, and autonomy. *Living as a nomad is one of the most empowering moves a woman can make.*

There were plenty of times I had doubts about getting on the road. It felt crazy and irrational ... why would I want to risk such a life-altering change, giving up my cozy apartment and most of my material possessions, to embrace a way of life I wasn't even sure I could handle?

When those fears reared up, I tuned into my Body Compass. *My Body Compass reading was so strong that it felt like there was an actual magnet in my body pulling me to get on the road.* It felt as if my body was moving of its accord and I was an observer watching myself go through the process of becoming a nomad. *Crazy, right!?* My ego and social-self went nuts, but when I listened to the inner guidance of my Body Compass, I knew it was coming from a profound, wiser part of me that was impossible to ignore.

The Dig Deeper exercises at the end of this chapter will give you more detailed instructions to explore and calibrate your own Body Compass, but you can find out right now what your Body Compass says about living as a nomad. Ask yourself;

"What do I feel in my body when I reflect on living as a nomad?"

Do you feel an answer in your body? (Not in your mind!)
What sensations come up in your body?
Where do you feel that answer in your body?
Does your body feel lighter, or heavier?
Do you have a little hum of excitement in your chest or abdomen, a sensation that feels stimulating, that makes you breathe a little faster, but doesn't exactly feel like fear?

Your Body Compass is unique from anyone else's, but the sensations of a positive direction will *feel good* in your body. Try the opposite, and think about never living as a nomad ... where do you feel that in your body? Do you feel contraction, or expansion? Are there any sensations you notice in your heart or gut?

Your unique wisdom will know if nomadic life is right for you, or not.

Each of us has a personalized set of *internal signals that give a yes or a no answer when we need guidance.* For some, a bad decision feels like a tightening in the gut combined with burning in the shoulders. For others, it might be a tingling sensation. The right choice may feel like a warmness in the face, or a light feeling somewhere else in the body.

Trusting those signals from our essential selves, in spite of outside pressure to conform, will lead us in the right direction. The Body Compass never lies, isn't influenced by what anyone else thinks, and is always right ... with the caveat that the sensations we're tuning into are actually the Body Compass, and not other strong emotions like love, excitement, or fear.

When I can't get a reading on my own Body Compass, it's usually because anxiety is over-riding my intuition. My partner Nancy and I recently weathered a tropical storm in Arizona, and we spent days before it hit trying to decide whether to move. I kept envisioning us getting stuck in a mud pit out in the forest, unable to evacuate if a road washed out. It felt like we should leave, but I couldn't tell whether I was feeling anxious about getting stuck, or if it was an accurate reading from my Body Compass. I collected as much information as I could from the local

69

rangers, sheriff's office, and weather forecasts … and the day before the storm hit, we made the decision to stay. It was a wet and miserable two days, but the decision was sound, and there were no muddy disasters!

There's no question that it takes courage to challenge the social self and listen instead to the quiet direction of our essential selves. Our fearful ego-self, as we've discussed in the previous chapter, will do anything to resist radical alterations to our life path! ***Our Body Compass can lead us to places that will challenge us to face our deepest fears, but will also lead to our most profound joy!***

Planning for nomadic life can feel overwhelming. We may deeply desire it, but fear and uncertainty can keep us stuck. There may be family involved that's not fully supportive, or we feel guilty for leaving. We might have a fear of being alone, or have valid financial obstacles. And let's not forget the purge … what do we sell, give away, store, discard or take along? Sorting through a lifetime of accumulated possessions is a daunting task! (Covered in Chapter 6!)

Remember the experiment with the card decks? Our body knows the truth long before the mind. The trick is to ignore fearful thoughts, even just for a moment, and tune into the quieter voice of our Body Compass.

You don't have to see where you're going to know where you're going!

Our path may not seem apparent, but consistently following those signals, like a set of headlights on a dark road, can lead us to our most content and happy life.

Once we know we're feeling the positive pull of our body compass, and not the negative repulsion of fear, we can stop saying maybe ... and say a hearty YES to the journey.

That conscious *YES* commits us, even if we can't yet see a clear path. Once we say *YES*, all of the little steps that bring us closer to our dreams will begin to come into focus. It doesn't mean everything changes overnight, but saying a clear *YES* awakens the life energy that propels us forward, and gathers the forces that help us on the way.

When we say yes, our dreams start to transition from something we're just thinking about, to reality flourishing in the physical world.

"When you are inspired by some great purpose, some extraordinary project, all your thoughts break their bonds; your mind transcends limitations; your consciousness expands in every direction; and you find yourself in a great, new and wonderful world." ~ Patanjali

In the Dig Deeper prompts for Chapter three, you'll learn how to find your own personal Body Compass.

DIG DEEPER: TUNE IN TO YOUR WILD GUIDE –
THE BODY COMPASS

"Think of a time when you felt electric. That's your
mojo. That's what's real. Everything else is fear or
doubt, but it's not truth. Your truth makes you feel
alive. What you know when you're inspired, that's
what's real." ~ Tama J Kieves

Are you driving yourself crazy trying to make a decision?
This exercise to *calibrate your Body Compass* will teach
you how to access your most enlightened wisdom, and
make decisions based on *what your authentic self really
wants.* Our Body Compass points us to our own True
North ... where we live as our most joyful and authentic
selves.

We discover our personal Body Compass by locating
sensations in our body connected to negative or positive
events.

Emotions Vs. Sensations.

Our body stores responses to life events, a physical imprint
on our body. Memories are accessed by our minds, but the
body also stores the *memories of physical reactions* to
those events. We find those responses by paying close
attention to sensations in the body.

Different from the intense *emotions* of excitement, love, or
fear, the Body Compass is experienced as *sensations* in the
body like cold hands, warm chest, relaxed shoulders, or

clenched jaw. Your body compass is a unique, personal *physical* response to life events.

Body Compass Exercise.

***IMPORTANT: For women who have unresolved trauma or PTSD, the Body Compass exercise can be a TRIGGERING EVENT. Stop if you find yourself getting overwhelmed.

Listed below are two ways to calibrate your Body Compass.

Body Compass Exercise #1.

To calibrate your Body Compass, you'll be doing a body scan to locate **sensations** in your body. The body scan is used in both Body Compass exercises.

Directions for a basic body scan: Close your eyes and move your attention to the space inside of your body, starting with your feet. Notice what *sensations* you feel in your feet, and then slowly work your way up through your legs, groin, stomach, gut, back, chest, shoulders, arms, hands, neck, head, face. ***You want to tune in to pure physical sensations in the body, not emotional reactions or thoughts about what you're feeling.*** You'll notice stronger sensations in some parts of your body, and in others, you may not feel anything.

The exercise below will teach you how to find your Negative Body Compass Reading, which is your "NO" answer, and your Positive Body Compass reading, which is your "YES" answer.

Doing the Negative Body Compass exercise can be uncomfortable, as you'll be bringing up the memory of a negative event. *Be sure to follow with the Positive Body Compass Exercise so you can end this exercise feeling with positive feelings.*

Directions for finding your Negative Body Compass.

First, take three deep relaxed breaths and let any thoughts drift away. You're aiming for a neutral feeling to begin.

1. Bring up a memory of something you'd describe as a negative experience in your life. If you've had trauma, DO NOT use the triggering event for this exercise.

2. Hold the negative memory in your mind, and recreate it as vividly as you can in your imagination. What did you see during the event? Hear? See? Taste? Smell? Touch? Spend a minute to bring the memory into sharp focus.

3. *While holding this vivid memory in your mind, do the body scan* as described above. Make a note of the sensations you feel in your body *while being present to this memory.* You'll be amazed to discover your body has its own memory!

4. When you're done, release the memory. Come back to the present moment by noticing what is around you right now. Look around and focus on what you see, hear, smell, taste, touch. Take three deep relaxing breaths.

What were the **sensations** you felt while imagining the negative memory? Note where you felt the top three or four strongest *sensations*, then give your Negative Body Compass a name. For example, a Negative Body Compass could be called Tight and Heavy, Terrible Yuk or Clenched Stomach ... be as creative as you like but use a name that you'll associate with your personal **Negative Body Compass.**

Your Negative Body Compass is your **"NO"** answer when you're looking for guidance.

Rate Your Negative Body Compass on a scale from 1-10, 1 being the least negative feeling and 10 being the absolute worst.

Name of Negative Body Compass

_____

Rating of Negative Body Compass

_____

Directions for Finding Your Positive Body Compass

Now using the *same process as above*, bring up a positive memory. Hold the positive memory in your mind, and using the body scan directions note the sensations in your body. *Name and rate your Positive Body Compass, using creative descriptions like Light and Centered, Calm Stomach, or Clear and Warm.*

Your Positive Body Compass is your **"YES"** answer when you're looking for guidance.

Name of Positive Body Compass

_____.

Rating of Positive Body Compass

Body Compass Exercise #2.

The next method is a shorter but less detailed way to calibrate your Body Compass.

Use this method to calibrate the negative or positive Body Compass.

Take three deep relaxed breaths and let your thoughts drift away. You're aiming for a neutral feeling to start.

1. Think of a negative or positive experience in your life. If you've had trauma, DON'T use the triggering event for this exercise.

2. Hold the negative or positive memory in your mind, and recreate it as vividly as you can. What did you see? Hear? Taste? Smell? Touch? Spend a minute to bring the memory into sharp focus.

3. This time you won't be using the body scan. Instead, _while holding the vivid memory in your mind,_ close your eyes and _feel the sensations_ within your body. Note the strongest sensations and where they're occurring in your body.

When you're done, release the memory. Come back to the present moment by noticing what is around you right now.

Look around and focus on what you see, hear, smell, taste, touch. Take three deep relaxing breaths.

What were the *sensations* you felt while imagining the negative or positive memory? Note where you felt the top three or four strongest *sensations*, then give your Negative or Positive Body Compass a name. For example, a Negative Body Compass could be called Tight and Heavy, Terrible Yuk, or Clenched Stomach … and your positive Compass could be Beautiful Light, Free and Sweet, or Centered and Cool … be as creative as you like but use a name that you'll associate with your personal Negative or Positive **Body Compass.**

Now that you've experienced your Body Compass, you can explore how it guides you to your wisdom. You can use your Body Compass to find your personal truth about any decision or situation!

Some people have difficulty naming their sensations. Here's a list to get you inspired.

Examples of POSITIVE SENSATIONS

Light

Expansive

Warm

Relaxed

Tingly

Airy

Clear

Bright

Fluid

Open

Examples of NEGATIVE SENSATIONS

Tight

Heavy

Clenched

Foggy

Pressure

Chilled

Gripping

Hard

Trembly

Numb

There are no wrong sensations. One Life Coaching client told me it felt like her feet were running, a very positive sensation for her.

The Body Compass, as taught by Martha Beck in her Life Coach Training, rates the Body Compass readings on a chart called the North-Star-O-Meter, with -10 being the worst sensation and +10 being the best.

This is the chart, Reprinted with Permission from Martha Beck Inc. Copyright Martha Beck, marthabeck.com.

North Star O-Meter

Make a list of words that describe the reactions, feelings, and gestures your body experiences when you imagine your worst-case scenario. These are the words you associate with your strongest negative feelings. List these words below the left side of the chart. Then make a list of the words that describe your strongest positive feelings and list them under the right side (under the positive numbers on the chart.)

Strongest Negative Feeling   Neutral   Strongest Positive Feeling

-10 -9 -8 -7 -6 -5 -4 -3 -2 -1   0   +1 +2 +3 +4 +5 +6 +7 +8 +9+10

Now that you have your Body Compass calibrated, here's how you can use it as a tool to make any decision in your life, large or small.

For example, one of the major decisions a nomad must make is their vehicle purchase. To use the Body Compass for this decision, first get into a relaxed neutral state. Fear, excitement, or any other intense emotions can interfere with Body Compass readings. Hold the image of purchasing a specific vehicle in your mind, and turn your attention to the space within your body. Try not to "think" the answer, let your body sensations come up without the mind interfering.

Do the sensations feel like your Positive Body Compass reading, or your Negative?

How would you rate the sensations on the chart? (see above) -10 to +10?

Where does your vehicle purchase rate on the chart, based on the strength of the sensations you're feeling?

Once you've calibrated your own Body Compass, you can use it to bypass the ego-fear and confusion of the mind, allowing you to make decisions based on your inner truth.

Experiment with the Body Compass on smaller decisions like what to have for lunch, or which road to take home. Practice learning this fantastic message system of your body.

(If you'd like further assistance from a Martha Beck Life Coach to calibrate your Body Compass, you can contact me through my social media accounts.)

From the words of Martha Beck, talking about our dreams: "Your body and emotions will tell you they're possible by yelling, "YES!" when you think about them".

"Though the gifts of wildish nature, come to us at birth, societies attempt to "civilize" us into rigid roles has plundered this treasure, and muffled the deep life-giving messages of our own souls. We become over-domesticated, fearful, uncreative, trapped."
~ Dr. Clarissa Pinkola Estes

CHAPTER FOUR: NAVIGATING THE ROCKY ROADS OF CHANGE

"It's in the struggle of life that we grow our wings."
~ Crystal Andrus

Having the burning desire to get on the road is a wonderful thing, but how the heck do we get from POINT A to POINT B, from having that wild-assed dream to making it a reality?

Becoming a nomad is an ongoing transition, from the time we nurture just a glimmer of the idea, to the time we become a full-fledged Wild Woman on the road. The process doesn't end when we finally launch … the transition continues emotionally, mentally and physically as the days and months roll on. From the physical adjustments of not living in a permanent shelter, to the emotional exploration of how we define ourselves as nomads, the mantra of becoming a nomad could be, "everything keeps changing!" The nomadic journey is ALL about change! As nomads, the neighborhoods where we park our living rooms change on a regular basis! One day we may be waking up to a cool shady primal forest, a few hours later we're baking in the hot desert sun!

In Chapter One we talked about having W.I.G.s, Wildly Improbable Goals, (a nomadic lifestyle definitely qualifies) but it's easy to get overwhelmed when we start to consider *ALL OF THE THINGS THAT HAVE TO GET DONE!* We're not just making a move from one home to another, we're changing a lifelong way of existence. Feelings of overwhelm can keep us stuck in THINKING too much, then freezing up, (analysis paralysis) holding us back from making any forward movement towards our dreams.

Here's the good news - understanding the process of change will help us get through it with our sanity. Knowledge is power!

With any significant life changes, there's a predictable cycle of emotional phases that we experience, whether we perceive the change is for the best, or not.

Called the Change Cycle by life coach and author Martha Beck, she compares the human process of change to the life cycle of a butterfly. This may sound like "airy-fairy-woo-woo stuff," but bear with me, this metaphor is a profoundly accurate description of the phases of *human* metamorphosis.

Whether it happens by choice or necessity, change is usually preceded by a catalytic event, something that either compels or forces us into a different life direction. A catalytic event usually leaves us asking ourselves, *"What in the hell is happening!???"* This catalytic event can be unexpected or planned, appearing as a crisis, an opportunity, or a transition.

This catalytic event could come as a shock, such as a divorce, changes in finances for the worst, or some other equally painful **crisis**. While it often is a crisis, it can also show up as an **opportunity** like a new job offer or mobile career - many women on the road are successful digital nomads and entrepreneurs. Although for most women retirement usually means a decrease in income, it can also be a perfect opportunity to finally grab our freedom and fulfill our wanderlust. Going through menopause, a **transition** many women in this lifestyle are familiar with, can be profoundly liberating, leaving us with a dramatically lowered tolerance for bullsh*t and a new-found desire for a meaningful life.

As we go through the life-changing catalytic event, things may fall apart around us, the beginning of the first phase of change, which Martha Beck describes as "Square One" of the change cycle. In the initial period after a catalytic event, we experience "dissolving, death and rebirth." Nothing is familiar, and we meltdown, right down to the core of our identity. In the life cycle of a butterfly, this is when the caterpillar completely dissolves inside the chrysalis. Amazingly, it doesn't then just morph into a butterfly, *but melts into an unrecognizable mass of cells.*

As we become nomads, we may go through this "dissolving" process multiple times. We dissolve a familiar way of life, purging of belongings, giving up dependency on modern conveniences, and ultimately our identity as a traditional house dweller. This mushy stage is often a time of grief and letting go. The life we once knew may be over, but the new life ahead of us is still just a mass of uncertainty. This is when it's time to take exceptional care of ourselves. On some days, it may be all we can do to just breathe.

Watching my mother decline and finally succumb to Alzheimer's Disease was a crisis that left me longing to live my life as authentically and joyfully as possible, and propelled me on a course of change that included ending a toxic marriage. Even though this was by choice, it was still emotionally painful to let go of a relationship, a home, and way of life.

This emotionally extreme phase of meltdown is ***absolutely necessary to pave the way for change.***

When we're in it, it feels like the confusion will never end, but eventually we get through the initial meltdown and start dreaming of a new life. Square Two of change, called "Dreaming and Scheming" by Martha Beck, is when we start imagining how things could be better. The butterfly isn't yet formed in the chrysalis, but still in the process of becoming. Hope arises, and this can be a liberating time as we explore visions of a new life. This is the phase when we're free to explore our Wildly Improbably Goals, W.I.G.s as we discussed in the first chapter, *without censoring*. When we tap into our imagination in this dreaming stage, spontaneous ideas may start popping up, and our daydreams often include details of our future life on the road!

When the dream has fully formed and we find ourselves doing the actual physical work to build it, we've entered Square Three. During this time, the butterfly labors to break free of the chrysalis, a crucial struggle that ensures its wings expand with circulating life fluids, allowing for impending flight. For humans, this is our Hero's Saga. We enter a time of exploring unknown territory, of trial and error, hard work, and building our knowledge and confidence. When something goes wrong it isn't considered a failure, but a valuable lesson that gets us even closer to success. It's been said that it takes 10,000 hours of practice to become a master at any skill, and becoming a nomad is no exception! When we first start out as nomads everything seems so much harder than we expected and our great ideas often don't work out! *THE STRUGGLE IS REAL!* Hang in there … the best is yet to come.

Eventually, we reach Square Four, Full Fight into the promised land! The butterfly is free and flying, and as humans, we've finally figured things out and are now making small adjustments to stay aloft. We easily maintain the dream, finally reaping the JOY, FREEDOM, and FULFILLMENT we knew in our heart was possible!

My own journey is a textbook example of this, going from a vague yearning that was only a half-formed dream, to planning, then doing, and finally now, living that dream.

These phases of change, called "Squares" by Martha Beck, go like this:

Square One: Meltdown. Death and rebirth, loss of identity and the familiar. (The caterpillar melts down inside the chrysalis.) Mantra: "I don't know what the hell is going on, and that's OK."

Square Two: Imagination/Dreaming and Scheming. After fully melting down, grieving, and letting go, new dreams start to appear, and a new life begins to feel possible. (The caterpillar starts reforming within the chrysalis.) Mantra: "There are no rules, and that's OK."

Square Three: Hero's Saga. Dreams now become a reality, and hard work ensues. (The caterpillar struggles to escape the chrysalis.) Mantra: "This is much harder than I expected, and that's OK."

Square Four: Full Flight, The Promised Land! All the work has paid off, and now the new life becomes established as the familiar. (The caterpillar is flying free!) Mantra: "Change is coming, and that's OK."

From caterpillar to butterfly … from initial meltdown and loss of the familiar, to dreaming and reforming, to struggling out of the chrysalis, to finally flying free … the cycle of the butterfly is an elegant metaphor for our human lives.

Part of my process included a premonition that my life would be changing. Although the mystery autoimmune illness still had me in its grip, in 2015 I'd managed to make it to our family's annual camping trip in the Adirondacks. I was unable to hike, swim, or do any of the outdoor activities that were dear to my heart, but just being outside for a week in the pristine forests of the Adirondacks filled me with the earth's healing energy.

I wrote in my journal back then, *"If I could live this way (outside in the wild) I'd be healed."*

That was the beginning of my dream.

In the year after that camping trip, I was consumed with the desire to live a mobile life on the road close to nature. It filled me with determination and set my imagination on fire!

By then I was seeing some small improvements in physical and cognitive functioning, and I dared to dream it might be possible. ***That dream wouldn't leave me alone!***

I began researching RV's, watched countless videos, read articles, bought books on nomad life, and soaked up information from bloggers and YouTubers who were heartily living the way of life I was craving. I discovered a mobile community across North America, many who were women, feeling the same nomadic calling.

At times, the fire of my dream would dim, and I'd settle back into the contentedness of my comfy, stationary life ... questioning why I would ever want to leave it ... but then the dream would catch fire again and ignite my soul.

Many women I've met on the road have similar stories, of dreaming and researching, sometimes for years, before finally fulfilling their nomadic dreams. We can nurture our vision until it's ready to be born into the world.

In early 2016 I wrote, *"I still want to be on the road. I could explore the Adirondacks from Spring to fall. The first thing is to attain a good vehicle, a great vehicle, that is mine."*

So there began the plan, born of the dreams.

I wrote about the cozy apartment I'd made my home: *"I love this place where I live, yet I feel such a restlessness. I want to just chuck it all and go. Is it the human spirit that wants to expand, grow, explore!?"*

And then I wrote the words that changed my life: ***"I surrender. I let the universe open the way to my true path."***

This powerful *letting-go* energy flipped the "on" switch to manifesting my dreams! Soon after writing those words I found the perfect vehicle, a mini-van that could easily be converted into a camper-van, and small enough for me to manage alone with the physical limitations of a chronic illness.

My dream now had wheels! It had all felt so distant up to that point, but now the dream had an actual physical manifestation! Even after I had my vehicle, I still had no solid plan. I almost couldn't believe I was so close to living what was just a crazy dream a few years before.

I was finally coming home to myself. I wasn't making a drastic change to please another person, or changing my lifestyle to fit society's idea of *who I should be.* With the self-acceptance I'd practiced over the years, I no longer needed outside approval to feel whole. It was totally ok that my dream only made sense to me.

I consciously pictured myself in awe-inspiring natural surroundings, adjusting easily, and experiencing beauty, health, and widening horizons. I imagined myself exploring the world, having miraculous encounters with other humans and the earth. (Little did I know I'd also meet the love of my life in the desert Southwest!)

I'd gone through the complete meltdown of my identity. After leaving the swing-world and my marriage, and then becoming ill and cocooning in my apartment, I was now starting to make plans for a new life!

My oldest daughter, (who is totally supportive) *said back then that my dream was crazy.* Not in a bad way crazy, but out of the norm crazy, and her sensible suggestion was to at least take a test spin and sleep one night in the van. It was a great idea … I threw an air mattress and a few supplies in the van and took an overnight trip to a local campground.

It was there any lingering doubts fled. I was one with the trees, the earth, the sky, the wildness that came to greet me. I knew then, I was home.

That very first night out was agony and ecstasy. I couldn't figure out how to shut off the ambient lighting inside the van, which stayed on when I locked the doors *from the INSIDE.* I made multiple trips climbing back and forth over the front seat trying to figure out the electronics, and somehow discovered I had to open and shut the driver's side door *from the inside* to get everything to power down. Then, there were the multiple pee trips during the night to the nearby campground toilets, a valuable learning experience! Exhausted and disoriented, I woke up several times during the night trying to figure out what I was doing in the back of a mini-van!

In that one night, I gained valuable information about what was needed to make the van comfortable, an indoor bathroom solution being high on the list. I was solidly in Square Three! There was plenty of work ahead of me, but I knew then, to the bottom of my toes, that it would be totally DO-ABLE.

A few months later I had a written plan, lists galore, and a spreadsheet of finances that included my simple van build and every camping supply I could think of. I picked a date to move out of the apartment, and a tentative launch date. I'd already been purging my belongings, and went to work selling or giving away what was left. (I did put a few things in storage which I got rid of 6 months later.) I moved in with my oldest daughter and her husband, at that time making their home my home base.

Solidly in Square Three, I moved out of my apartment in March of 2017, and in June 2017 launched with a summer trip into the Adirondacks, and even with the swarms of mosquitos in that summer of rain, I loved it! By the end of the season, I was all in. To continue van dwelling I knew I'd have to get out of the Northeast for the winter, and as I considered my options, felt a strong pull to the Southwest. I headed West to Arizona in October of 2017 as a solo female van dweller, fulfilling one of the most wonderful and frightening dreams of my life!

I'd spent years in the dreaming phase, from dreaming a crazy idea, to working to make the dream real, to finally launching in 2017. Meltdown, dreaming and reforming, struggle, and then on to full flight!

The change cycle started all over again when I hit the road. I struggled with my body's limitations, and at times things were not as rosy as it had all seemed when I was dreaming away in my comfy apartment … *but I felt ALIVE like never before.*

Imagining myself on the road, I wrote in my journal, *"My body has been broken, I'm disabled by the standards of this society and government, yet, I can feel who I am on the road. I love her. She is Strong. Resilient. Healthy. Serving. Awake. In love with the world. Grateful to be on this earth, experiencing this earth. The dream ignites again and burns away doubt and discouragement. I am ALREADY THAT PERSON! Remember that! Remember her!"*

Now I've become that woman I wrote about, the woman who was waiting to be reborn.

I'm now flying free in Square Four. After many, MANY months and years of trial and error, I feel confident in my routine as a Wild Woman On The Road. I've hit my 10,000 hours of practice, but I've also learned that by its very nature, a nomad's life is about constant change … we cycle through all the squares of the change cycle over and over again!

There's no significant change in our lives that doesn't come with a measure of pain and grief. ***Don't let fear of this emotional distress hold you back!***

Every woman alive has been born with an abundance of strength and courage to deal with the emotional challenges of change. Take time to consider what you'll be looking back on at the end of your life. Let's not miss out on our best lives out of the fear of change! In the end, we'll regret the adventures we didn't have.

At times, I've wept with the agony and ecstasy of this dream. My family, my heart, is at times long-distance across the many miles, yet I would never go back to my old life. Now I'm the traveling adventure Grandma. I can live with that!

> *"In daily life, there is an inner transition I can consciously practice. This is the transition from fear to faith." ~ Julia Cameron*

Where you are in your own Change Cycle? In the Dig Deeper work for this chapter, I'll share some specific tools to help you navigate the transitions of your life.

Credit: Martha Beck for all info re: Change Cycle.

DIG DEEPER: AVOIDING THE PERILS OF GETTING STUCK IN LIMBO-LAND

"Today allow yourself to have your dreams. Be "unrealistic" and believe that big joy is coming down the pike for you. Why not bet on your good instead of your failure? It's always those who are "unrealistic" that change reality in the end." ~ Tama J. Kieves

So how do we survive the cycles of change in our lives, and not get stuck in one place forever? Even the acute pain of grief eventually becomes a passage, and hopefully not a place we've taken up permanent residence. The following tools will give you the understanding to survive, thrive and move on in each "square" of the change cycle.

Credit Martha Beck Inc for all info re: Change Cycle.

SQUARE ONE TOOLS.

Square One: Meltdown. Death and rebirth. Butterfly inside the chrysalis melting into "goo." Square One is where you are after any major life change, usually a catalytic event. (See Chapter Four.)

The key word for this phase is **REST**. Don't make any big decisions in the meltdown stage, unless you absolutely must.

During this time of intense emotions, the body and mind require more rest than seems reasonable.

This isn't a phase of DO-ing. If we're a fixer and problem solver (CONTROL FREAK = Me) it can be a challenge to sit still with our emotions and ride it out. This is our opportunity to practice radical acceptance.

1. During this often painful time in the change cycle, it's crucial we practice excellent *self-care and healthy comfort measures.* Curl up with a soft blanket. Find some natural support like herbal tea. (I swear by essential oils, including CBD oil.) Take more naps. Give yourself permission to check out emotionally, to binge-out on Netflix, or treat yourself to a decadent dessert, but be careful not to numb out under the guise of self-care. We have to FEEL IT TO HEAL IT!

2. Reach out to supportive friends or family. Talking to a counselor or life coach is an invaluable investment.

3. Allow the flow of grief and other intense feelings. It's been said that strong emotions like grief come in 90-second waves, and eventually these waves, like ocean waves breaking against the sand, will melt away. It seems counterintuitive to immerse ourselves in grief, but allowing our feelings full expression frees us from getting stuck in them longer than necessary.

4. Don't forget to journal! Journaling is a proven therapeutic practice.

Practical exercises:

At times of overwhelm, remember to practice the breathing exercises and the loving kindness mantra discussed in chapter two.

Stay in the present moment. In this first messy phase of change, it can be normal to be immersed in worry. Focusing on the present moment can help ease the anxiety of uncertainty.

Try this exercise, called 5 4 3 2 1, to help ground you in the present moment and ease anxiety:

Look around the room you're in and identify 5 things you see.
Next, identify 4 things you hear.
Then, identify 3 things you feel. (your shoes on your feet, a watch on your wrist, etc.)
Now, 2 things you smell. (The air. Your shampoo.)
Finally, 1 thing you taste. (Even if it's just your tongue.)

Remind yourself that THIS TOO SHALL PASS. It will, and you will survive and thrive.

SQUARE TWO TOOLS.

Square Two: Dreaming and Scheming. Re-formation. Butterfly assembling from the mass of "goo." The intense pain and confusion of Square One is diminishing.

The key word for this phase is *ATTENTION.*

In this phase, your soul, your inner self, higher self, or whatever you call the source of your deepest wisdom, will express itself through your imagination, guiding you to your new life.

Pay attention to what LIGHTS YOU UP. Tune in to your Body Compass as we discussed in Chapter One. Notice what's lighting up your positive Body Compass sensations.

Pay attention to what visually attracts you. Make a vision board. It sounds like woo -woo, but it can clarify our deepest desires. Flip through magazines, and WITHOUT THINKING about it, cut out anything that your eye is drawn to, even if it doesn't make sense. Glue the images on a poster board, and put it where you'll see it every day.

Notice your daydreams and night dreams. This is another place our souls can give us clues about the next steps!

Remember, there's nothing you have to commit to in this stage. Let your mind be free to play with possibilities, and to pay attention to what makes you feel the most excited.

The Ideal Day Exercise.

The ideal day exercise is a chance to let your imagination take you into your future. To do this exercise, allow yourself to enter into a daydream about your perfect day. If you're thinking about becoming a nomad, make it about that. First, imagine waking up in the morning, when you open your eyes, what do you see? Where are you? What do you see out the window? Who, if anyone, is with you? What do you have for breakfast? What do you do after breakfast? What does your living space look like? Go through a complete day from morning to bedtime, and imagine as many details about this ideal day in your ideal life as you can. How do you feel in this ideal day? Are you happy? Comfortable? Scared?

Your ideal day exercise is just for fun, but it may give you surprising clues about your heart's desires.

 Journal what comes up, imagination can help us navigate our future!

Ideal Day Exercise Credit: Martha Beck

Chart Your Course.

One of the most powerful exercises I've ever done is to Chart The Course. I used it to chart a course to my life coaching career, thinking it was off in the future somewhere, and two weeks later an opportunity came out of nowhere! I could never have predicted it in a million years. The Planned Parenthood where I'd worked for 20 years was restructuring its organization, and I was suddenly out of a job, and unexpectedly free to start my own business! There's something about writing our goals down that sets thing in motion and rallies the forces in the universe.

Here's how to chart your course. Get a letter size piece of blank paper and turn it sideways. On the very left side of the paper, make a small box and label it "Where I am now." Now, on the very right side, draw a small box and label it with your W.I.G., your Wildly Improbably Goal as covered in chapter one. Now go back to the left side, where you are now, and make another small box to the right of the first one, and connect the boxes with a line. *In that second box put the very next little teeny tiny step you need to take towards your goal.* It could be subscribing to a YouTube channel that promotes women van dwellers, like CheapRVliving, or getting a book out of the library on nomad life. Now go to the next box to the right of that …and the next … the next … filling each box across the page until you get to the final box on the right of the page, your W.I.G.

Now, start taking all of those little "turtle steps, one step at a time!"

If you're like most women, there's always a long list of "things to be done" bouncing around in your head. Really there's ever only ONE thing to be done, and that's the one thing to do in the present moment. Do one thing in the moment. When that's done, then do the next thing.

What is your ONE thing that you can do today?

Try not to jump ahead in your mind to mull on the future, stay present and DO THAT ONE THING.

Don't forget to check in with your Body Compass. Tune in to your inner wisdom as you consider each step along your journey!

SQUARE THREE TOOLS

Square Three: The Hero's Saga. Emerging. Hard work! Butterfly struggling to emerge from the chrysalis. This is the Square where dreams start to become reality in the physical world.

The key word for this phase is ***IMPLEMENTATION.***

You've survived the meltdown of Square One. You've been dreaming about your new life, have done all the research, and allowed your soul's vision to guide you.

If you've done the previous exercise to Chart Your Course, you may have already taken some turtle steps to implement your dream.

Now it's time to get to WORK!

Here's the most important thing you need to remember for Square three:

EXPECT FAILURES!

Your dreams have been invaluable guidance, but it can be a rude awakening to experience real-world problems far removed from your idyllic visions. And that's OK.

When your beautiful ideas don't go as planned, know that *THIS IS SUPPOSED TO HAPPEN!* You'll be thinking, "this is all much harder and complicated than I thought it would be" … but remember Martha Beck's mantra for this phase: "THIS IS HARDER THAN I THOUGHT IT WOULD BE, AND THAT'S OK."

When plans go out of wack, return to the basics of Square One and Square Two. Practice self-care and get enough rest. Use your imagination and problem-solving skills to move on to a new plan!

Remember to use your Body Compass to guide you!

When failures throw you back into Square One and Square Two … remember that becoming a nomad is a steep LEARNING CURVE.

It goes like this:

1. I've got a dream!
2. I can do this dream!
3. Get to work on the dream!
4. This doesn't F'ing work!
5. Learn a lesson, dream and scheme some more, enlist brilliant problem-solving skills, and figure out what does work! Try again!

Remember your big WHY! Get inspired again. If you journaled about your WHY after reading chapter one, go back and read your journal!

Go get fresh inspiration and ideas from nomadic YouTubers, Websites, and Facebookers. Google what other nomads are doing to solve your problem. Engage with other nomads on forums. There is so much help and support out there for us!

SQUARE FOUR TOOLS

Square Four: Full Flight. Fully Formed. New Identity, New Life. The butterfly is now flying! You've made it!

The key word for this phase is **MAINTENANCE.**

If you've gotten this far in the Change Cycle, congratulations! You've successfully navigated the first 3 phases of change, and now you're ready to reap the payoff!

You need only small adjustments in your routine now, and you continue to make minor improvements in the quality of your life. You're flying, enjoy it!

Expect change to happen again!

"It's been my experience that at the very moment I feel like giving up, I'm only one step from a breakthrough. Hang on long enough and circumstances will change, too. Trust in yourself, your dream and spirit."
~Sarah Ban Breathnac

CHAPTER FIVE: NOMADISM AND THE CHALLENGES OF THE HERO'S JOURNEY

"Going Back Into Your Wild Nature Heals The Wild Nature Of The World." ~ Martha Beck

You've spent months if not years researching nomad life. You've dreamt and planned and worked your ass off to reach your launch day. You've watched every beautiful panoramic scene on YouTube, poured over the perfect Instagram moments, and memorized every route you're longing to travel. Your vehicle is finally road-ready, you're filled with intoxicating anticipation, envisioning yourself a free and happy nomad, your head filled with beautiful visions of the sights you'll see and the people you'll meet.

The time finally comes, and you're on the road! You've made it! You've planned and purged and navigated all the obstacles and you feel a thrilling emotional high to finally achieve your dream! You've done it!

Sometime after that, chances are good that the extreme high of your launch will be followed by an equally extreme low, probably sooner than later. You'll get burned out. You'll have times of worry and overwhelm. If you're a solo traveler, you may find yourself getting lonely or depressed. Thoughts of quitting might start nagging at you, or you may start wondering if you're really cut out for the nomadic lifestyle. You might get homesick for modern conveniences, or have any number of newfound struggles you couldn't foresee. You might start questioning your life choices, and wonder why nomadic life isn't as euphoric as

you thought it would be. The good news: THIS IS ALL
TOTALLY NORMAL!

There seems to be a strange occurrence for most nomads
that things go wrong when they first start out. It's almost
like the energy of the old life has to shake lose to make
room for the energy of the new life … and things in our
vehicles, psyches and bank accounts get broken and
shaken up. I call it Nomad Boot Camp and you can read
about it more on my website:
Cosmicnomadvoyager.com/nomad-boot-camp/

The decision to enter nomadic life throws us into nothing
less than a classic hero's journey. It starts when the hero
feels strangely compelled to depart from familiar
surroundings and enter a new and strange land. As we
traverse this unfamiliar land of the hero's journey,
encountering trials and adventure on the way, we confront
the darkness lurking in the unknown, and ultimately in
ourselves. Eventually, we learn to skillfully navigate this
unfamiliar territory, discovering our hero selves along the
way, and are reborn with the renewed confidence and
strength we've acquired on our journey. In the classic
hero's journey, the hero returns home from the land of
adventures - for women nomads, we're free to finally
return home to our Wild Women Selves.

After talking to other women on the road, "listening" in on
online forums, and experiencing my own turbulent ups and
downs, I've seen that the hero's journey for women is not
just physical, but played out in our rich emotional
landscapes. We traverse winding paths in the mountains
and valleys of our emotions, especially in the beginning of

our journey, and I'm convinced that some of these emotional swings are in part the process of detoxing from our traditional Westernized way of life. Good news: HANG IN THERE, IT GETS BETTER!

Our beautiful dreams are sacred, they keep us motivated … without them we'd never stretch ourselves, they're the fuel that keeps us moving in the direction of our wildest imagination. While dreams are the fuel, the realities of living on the road can sometimes end up being a full-stop rude awakening from the dream. Before I got on the road, I had visions of being the blissed-out hippie chick on the road, meditating and doing yoga in nature every day, but the reality is, some days of my nomadic life have me feeling more like a deranged lunatic than a tranquil Buddha.

As we all know, sh*t happens.

That's not to say there won't be days of bliss, and they certainly get more frequent the longer you've practiced being a nomad, but there's a surprising amount of non-blissful stuff to deal with. (I haven't yet reached the enlightenment stage where I only experience bliss!) You've probably heard the expression, "Life is what happens while we're making other plans," and there couldn't be a more valid description of the life of a nomad!

The day of my launch I was ecstatic to be finally getting on the road. The van build was complete, the fun Amazon shopping sprees were over, and all the supplies, gadgets and groceries were ready to go. What I didn't predict were the hours it would take to load everything up. It was pushing late afternoon before I headed out for my very first destination, a free boondocking site in the Adirondack foothills. Recommended by my mechanic, his words were, "easy to find" and "look for the sign saying, "Free Camping." *HAH!*

I drove around in circles for hours, using up the afternoon daylight looking for that damn sign … which turned out to be a faded slab of wood hidden deep in the bushes. Yep, I'd found it, but driving into an overgrown dirt path, I was looking up at a very steep, very rocky, poorly maintained "road" into the woods. Feeling desperate and a bit reckless, I gunned the Green Beastie … and didn't make it two feet up the hill. Thankfully my first day out didn't end up stuck with a flat tire on that rocky trail!

My grand plan flew out the window. *Lesson number one: always have a backup plan!* After being on the road for a while now, I've come to realize the importance of this lesson!.

I was exhausted, but dammit … I wasn't turning around. Not willing to give in to defeat, I checked into a nearby (and expensive!) paid campground.

I was so fatigued that after I cooked my dinner, I couldn't eat. Lying in my van bed that night, I had an all-out, think-I'm-gonna-die panic attack … partly triggered by the pretty fabric I'd hung over the bed that gave me never experienced before, full-blown claustrophobia. Fun times! The pretty fabric came down the next day. *(Lesson number two: decorative isn't always practical!)* In fact, some of the most successful female van dwellers I've met put  the practical before the decorative. That's not to say they haven't added personal touches, but the most decked out living quarters doesn't necessarily mean the most livable. I've since removed curtains that made the nightly routine of putting up the reflectix a total cluster-f*ck, added and subtracted bins and baskets and storage carts, and given up on having a picture-perfect Instagram van. You can see from the picture my "organization" went right out the window. Thankfully, I've evolved! While the basic organization of my van has stayed the same, like where I put my flashlights, toothbrush, meds or other daily necessities, it's undergone many a metamorphosis since launch day. Most likely, you'll go through a similar process. You can check out the evolution of my van on my website, cosmicnomadvoyager.com. Look for the blog post about Van Shui!

I spent four days at that paid campground, too freakin' stubborn to give up. I thought I'd carefully organized the van, but couldn't find anything when I needed it, keeping me constantly frustrated and the inside of the van in disarray. (See picture!) I was forced to rethink the practical aspects of existing comfortably in that small space, and my first major van purge took place the next day. While I agree that research and preparation are essential, there is an almost universal experience among nomads that **no matter how much we prep, we'll never know exactly what we're doing until we're on the road!** *Be prepared to feel uncomfortable for the first couple of weeks, or even months!*

After those four days, I went back to my then home base to recover. Going back out the next week, I had a more realistic view of what I was getting into, now with some lessons under my belt. Having a chronic illness it was crucial to pace myself, and I'd learned that the simplest tasks in sticks-and-bricks, like cooking, cleaning, and hygiene, take twice as long to get done in the nomadic lifestyle. Especially in a van! Keeping our *mental and physical energy* up for that adjustment can be a challenge at first, and the perfect YouTube videos and Instagram moments rarely include information on how physically demanding and time-consuming this lifestyle can be. **Even the most physically fit nomad must take time out for rest, or risk getting burned out.** (Tips to avoid burnout in the next Dig Deeper exercises.)

My next trip a few weeks later turned out to be another fiasco ... my destination, a dispersed camping area in Lake George, NY, was so thick with mud that I couldn't get the Uplander into a campsite for the night. It was pushing sunset when I called the rangers at the NYSDEC (New York State Department of Environmental Conservation) for recommendations, and although I'd applied for the

New York State disabled camping permit allowing easy  access to handicapped campsites, it wasn't yet approved. Thankfully, the ranger was kind enough to give me the gate-code for a nearby site, just for the night. Like trying to get through the mud in the road, I was slowly slogging along, taking one step forward and two frustrating steps backward in my quest for nomadic life.

I'd wanted to stay closer to home base to start out, but after two fails, decided to head out farther from my safety net. I drove up to Forked Lake in the Adirondacks where my family camped every summer. With no amenities except an outhouse and a nearby clean water source at the boat landing, (which I now consider uber-luxuries) I camped for two days in one of the few drive-in sites on the lake. The caretaker there guided me to free dispersed campsites nearby in the Long Lake area, and I spent the next two weeks boondocking next to a beautiful Adirondack stream. It was one of the wettest Adirondack seasons in recent years, I was getting eaten alive by swarms of mosquitos, black flies and no-see-ums, but in spite of my daily outfit of mosquito netting, rain gear, and mud boots, (see the picture of my Adirondack fashion statement) I was elated to be finally living my dream! I *finally* felt like I was on my way!

After finally feeling like I was on my feet, I headed further up into the Adirondacks for the summer, solo boondocking up and down the Route 30 corridor at free dispersed campsites in Long Lake, Horseshoe Lake, Cedar River Flow, and Little Clear Pond, as well as a few days here and there at paid campgrounds like Forked Lake and Lake Eaton. My confidence soared, and I began to find my groove. I WAS FINALLY DOING IT!

I thought years of solitary living had prepared me for solo van life, but I was flat out wrong. My wild dream of van dwelling in the Adirondacks was finally a reality, but episodes of depression and anxiety started making a regular appearance, something I thought I'd resolved years ago. I was surprised to feel bouts of loneliness, which I hadn't experienced living alone in my apartment for eight years. The excitement of dreaming, prepping, and finally getting on the road was wearing off, and now the hard work of (then solo) living as a nomad had begun. Nomadic life is a wildly beautiful opportunity for deep healing of our wild feminine souls … but as my partner Nancy recently said, "this lifestyle isn't for the fainthearted!"

As nomads, we may change our lives and locations, but we can never escape ourselves.

I was loving van dwelling, but the onset of depression and anxiety forced me into deeper self-examination. I was navigating unexplored emotional, mental, physical and spiritual territory. The learning curve of nomadic life can seem overwhelming at first. There are constant demands on our time and energy just to make life comfortable on the road, and we're forced to deal with conditions we just aren't used to, like regulating our body temperature when the weather is too cold or too hot, keeping up with supplies of potable water, or taking care of daily hygiene without flush toilets or showers. I loved the convenience of my Thetford Porta-potti, but figuring out where to dump the damn thing was a nuisance! The level of constant uncertainty, of practicing new skills, and being at the bottom of the learning curve, was *exhausting.*

The weather was a nonstop factor camping in the Adirondacks, as it is in most places for a nomad, and that year was one of the rainiest spring/summer seasons in Adirondack history. On more than one occasion, I threw dripping wet tarps into the van when it was time to move! I learned to track the weather forecast, and be prepared to move on sooner if my 14-day camping limit landed on a day with rain predictions. It also didn't help my mental health much to be dealing with constant rain and too few sunny days.

When people said they envied me, I laughed, thinking of the mental, emotional and physical stamina this lifestyle was demanding of me. While being an experienced camper somewhat prepares us for nomadic living, there's a big difference between camping for a few weeks, and living outdoors permanently as a nomad.

Another major adjustment was having little to no cell signal at some sites in the Adirondacks. It didn't take long to learn how much I absolutely hated that. While I can't always avoid it, to this day it's one of my first considerations in choosing locations!

Detoxing from Modern Life

Before becoming a nomad, I hadn't owned a TV for years, but had a daily habit of spending hours on my laptop - watching Netflix, browsing social media, and having the internet at my fingertips 24/7.

I was no different than most civilized modern Westerners sedated by a steady state of consuming ... whether it be TV, internet media, material goods, information, or food. We're encouraged to keep consuming, stay employed and work hard enough to enable our continued contribution to ~~society~~ consumerism, all with the ultimate goal of making more money to spend on the constant upgrades, forcing us into a cycle of perpetual consumption. To keep us spinning on this hamster wheel, we're kept in unnatural emotional states - sedated and tired just enough to keep us from rebelling, but stimulated and motivated just enough to enable us to keep working. All the while, we're exposed to a daily, carefully curated stream of media that's specifically researched and designed to convince us we need to keep on consuming and upgrading. With this never-ending *external* bombardment of mood-altering media, we end up without the energy, time, or desire to get familiar with the *ever-shifting weather of our normal, human, inner emotional climate.*

We get used to a few "normalized" emotional states - happiness, fear, sadness, desire, love, hatred - without ever knowing the internal ebb and flow of the more

subtle and layered feelings and emotions contained within our "human" being. Fear can have sub-states, including alarm, terror, mortification or panic. Happiness can encompass feelings of delight, to jubilation. Anger can be a smokescreen for shame, shame can make us feel humiliated, alienated, or insecure. As humans we're capable of experiencing complexities of emotion so personal they defy definition.

In our modern lifestyle, it isn't considered valuable, or normal, to put aside time to just sit with the complexities of our feelings. There are constant distractions from our internal emotional landscape ... from TV and the multimedia of the internet, to the on-call demands of our cell phones, night or day.

Detoxing from the sedation of consumerism is one of the most profound effects of becoming a nomad, and at times, one of the most challenging.

Getting on the road removed me from the hypnotic effects of long hours of daily screen time, and withdrawing from my internet habit forced me to face the authentic emotional, mental and physical ups and downs of being *fully human*. The healing I was looking for in this lifestyle presented itself with an unanticipated onset of emotional pain, an experience I suspect is common for many women on the road. I also had a broken heart missing my kids and grandkids, who'd before been the center of my life and just a short drive away. It seemed that the price of my freedom was to be paid in part with waves of grief.

And the anxiety! Anxiety had been no stranger in my life, but I'd always been in denial over it … minimizing the role it played in my life experiences. I'd experienced a spike in anxiety when I moved out of my apartment and in with my daughter and her family, but chalked it up to moving from a quiet, solitary life, to the chaos of my daughter's lively family, her two kids, dogs, gerbils, other random critters, and noisy visitors. When the anxiety continued on down the road, I was forced to face the reality that anxiety was an emotional fixture in my internal landscape.

I'd felt joyous and excited to finally be getting on the road, but in the weeks after my launch was surprised by the intense emotional ups and downs of nomadic life. I was finally living my dream, but now there were days when not only did I feel depressed, but I was also depressed that I felt depressed, a vicious cycle of uncertainty and self-doubt. After the many years of therapy for childhood trauma, dedication to personal growth, intense healing and self-acceptance, I thought I'd left all that behind. Here I was a Master level Reiki Practitioner and a Certified Martha Beck Life Coach for Women … but found myself struggling for emotional balance in my new life as a nomad.

Eventually, the emotional difficulties became an opportunity for deeper healing. Once again, I was learning that healing isn't linear … more like a spiral steadily rolling forward. We heal layer by layer, going deeper and deeper as we move forward, and nomadic life was the perfect catalyst for the next level of healing.

This cycle of healing led me into another profound level of love and acceptance of myself, exactly who I am, "flaws" and all. I came to accept that I would have times of anxiety, loneliness, and depression on the road, *but it was all completely worth the intense feelings of freedom and joy that I ALSO felt!* Thankfully the depression resolved after a few months, and my anxiety levels came down. I still have infrequent bouts of anxiety, but my mood has stabilized, and feelings of contentedness and confidence have steadily grown. My new normal is to feel deeply all the ups and downs, the high joys and the low frustrations, and be willing to ride the waves as they roll on in my internal ocean of being.

You WILL Experience Emotional Ups and Downs. Being a nomad requires emotional perseverance.

I'm still not walking around all ecstatic and Buddha-like, as I'd pictured myself in visions of nomadic life, but this is what I've figured out: *Sometimes we just have to stubbornly hang on!*

After living in a culture of conveniences, there's an adjustment period before we get used to our NEW NORMAL on the road. *It took persistence, stubbornness and a willingness to endure discomfort on every level of being ... physical, emotional, mental and spiritual ... before a stable level of happiness finally kicked in.*

It took months to feel remotely capable on the road, but now, things that felt like a struggle in the beginning are just routine. Starting out, putting up the reflectix in my van windows at night seemed like an exhausting, mind-bending project … now it's a piece of cake.

Over time we develop new "muscle memory" to accomplish the tasks of van dwelling, which like any new skill takes *persistence and repetition.* If it's true that becoming a master of anything takes 10,000 hours, we'll have the basic routine down in a few months … but the learning curve for lasting success is a long-term investment. New neural pathways must form in the brain to become successful at any skill, and living as a nomad definitely qualifies as a challenging skill!

I realized how far I'd come when I went back East to finish up some business after 10 months on the road. Going back to living in traditional housing for a few weeks, I was concerned about losing some of my hard-earned nomadic skills, but I'm happy to report that when I got back on the road, I still had it! It was almost effortless to pick up where I'd left off in my nomadic routine!

Once women get through the initial struggle and start feeling, "I've got this" they commonly say, "I'll never go back!" Our natural emotional endurance and fierceness as women are powerful allies in our nomadic journey.

Without a traditional home, possessions, and routines of Western life to define our identity, we're forced to come face to face with our authentic human self.

The road doesn't provide an easy escape for our problems, to the contrary, the nomad life becomes a mirror for unresolved issues. The one common denominator in our lives is OURSELVES. We've all heard the saying, "Wherever you go, there you are."

If we're running from problems, thinking we'll leave it all behind on the road, we're in for an unpleasant shock. Any unhealed issues, wounds, or problems we're running from will stubbornly join us as co-pilots. If our coping mechanism for emotional pain has been to run away, where are we going to run if we're already on the road? If our coping mechanism has been to numb out, how will we cope when we're forced to deal with the challenges of nomadic life as they happen in front of us in real time?

Despite the struggles, the one thing I've consistently felt on the Nomad journey right from the beginning is that *I AM ALIVE - I AM LIVING!*

Becoming a nomad taught me how important it is for my mental health and self-worth to be able to *accept myself just as I am*, anxiety and all. Being able to accept my quirky self has made it even more enjoyable to meet other interesting, quirky people who've chosen a life on the road! Being a confirmed introvert, I learned that being friendly and engaging with the humans that crossed my path, from store clerks to other nomads, gave me a feeling of connection that helped me not feel so isolated. As time went on and I started connecting to the nomadic community, especially in the Southwest, I felt more accepted than when I was living "normally" in the Northeast for the first 59 years of my life! And to top it off, after many years of dedicated singleness, I met and fell in love with my partner Nancy, another solo van-dweller. You never know what's going to happen on the road!

I've never before felt so completely whole.

It seems like there's a high percentage of nomads, and especially women on the road, who've experienced trauma, dysfunctional childhoods, depression, anxiety, and other mood disorders, but if anything, those conditions push us into finding what we didn't have ... wholeness, love, and a tribe that accepts us unconditionally. Many of us, myself included, discover self-acceptance born from the nomadic life like we've never experienced before.

It's been a truly joyful experience to meet other nomadic women experiencing similar journeys ... and it blows my mind how elegantly we're doing it! We as women are stronger and more capable than we've been taught to believe. *Being on the road serves up powerful lessons on just how capable we are!*

So ... why would we become nomads, throwing ourselves into this radical life, with so much possible turmoil? *Because we know in our hearts that the payoff is PRICELESS.*

When things get difficult, remember to reflect on your "why" as discussed in the first chapter. Just thinking about going back to apartment living makes me shudder ... I could be back there sitting comfortably in an apartment under a roof and four walls, stuck there after paying a pile of bills ... or ... *I can be out here claiming my freedom and seeing the world!* For me, remembering this always puts any temporary difficulties into perspective!

Being a nomad is an opportunity to really live life, to see what's around the next corner, to have experiences and meet people we'd never encounter sitting in one place. Embedded in those very experiences are the golden opportunities to discover ourselves again and again.

Becoming a nomad is a precious opportunity to define a new relationship with ourselves, and with life itself, a gift some people will never get to experience. (Thanks, Dennis Winn for sharing those words of wisdom!)

As fellow Life Coach Dani W Fake (yes, her real name) said in a Facebook post, "I'm Alive. Not heart-beating, lung-breathing little "a" alive, but Big "A" soul-level Alive."

Living as a nomad is our chance to be SOUL-LEVEL ALIVE!

"We must be willing to let go of the life we planned so as to have the life that is waiting for us."
~ Joseph Campbell

The next Dig Deeper exercises will give you tools to deal with the inevitable emotional and mental challenges that come up on the road.

DIG DEEPER: GET SUPPORT FOR YOUR HERO'S JOURNEY

"When I dare to be powerful, to use my strength in the service of my vision, then it becomes less and less important whether I am afraid." – Audre Lorde

1. DISCOVER YOUR EMOTIONAL TOOLBOX.

Living on the road as a nomad requires certain strengths, most of which have little to do with physical strength. Suanne Carlson, the director of the Women's RTR and H.O.W.A. (Homes On Wheels Alliance), has coined this acronym: **I. F.I.T.** - describing strengths that especially benefit nomads on the road:

I. = Independence
F. = Flexibility
IT. = Intuition

Take a minute to reflect on how and where you've displayed those qualities in your life.

While these qualities are especially important, when we take time to reflect, every one of us has a toolbox full of other strengths that have served us well in life.

Do you have a boundless perseverance that others may call stubbornness? Are you a confident, outspoken woman, which may have earned you the honor of being called a bitch? Maybe you're an a**-hole whisperer and have a magic touch with difficult people. Maybe you're a survivor of multiple adverse situations in your life, and you've learned to adapt, and even eventually thrive in difficult times.

Thinking about life challenges that you've already dealt with, what are some personal attributes that helped you get through them? If you aren't sure, ask a close friend or trusted family member what strengths they see in you. These strengths are invaluable in your life as a nomad! Set aside a few minutes to take inventory of your "Emotional Toolbox." These are your personal strengths that will serve you well as a nomad. Here's an example of mine:

EMOTIONAL TOOLBOX

OPTIMISM

PERSISTENCE/STUBBORNNESS

FLEXIBILITY

ADAPTABILITY

FAITH (NON-RELIGIOUS)

COURAGE

PROBLEM SOLVER

2. FIND YOUR COMMUNITY.

You're not alone on the road. Nomadic women are increasing exponentially, and with the convenience of social media, it's easier than ever to find your tribe. Be willing to reach out and ask for support, most nomadic women are more than eager to help a fellow nomad in need! As another female van dweller, says, **"Although we are often solo travelers, we are NOT alone in our journeys!" - Kit Vantastic**

In this digital world, we have the advantage of finding our tribe online, before we even get out on the road! Here's a list of some of the social media groups I've found helpful. (For a more complete list: Resource section at the end of the book.)

RVing women. Yearly paid membership. Women Only. Mostly geared for women with RVs.

Fabulous RVing Women Facebook group. Not just for RVs, includes all types of nomadic travel: Fabulous RVing Women FRVW

HomeOnWheelsAlliance.org. (HOWA) This is the non-profit that grew out of Bob Wells' work. Financial help for nomads, van builds, caravans, and the yearly gathering of the RTR and WRTR.

CheapRVLiving.com Bob Wells' website, founder of the RTR. Invaluable information on everything possible in the nomadic lifestyle.

Other Facebook Groups: (search Facebook to find) These groups may come and go, but if you do a search you can find the newest groups.

VanDwellers FaceBook: Live In Your Van

Mini-Van Campers

RTR Chatter

LGBT Nomads

Rainbow Nomads

Solo Female VanLife

Frugal Full-Time RVers.

Make sure to stay in touch with the community and support systems you already have in place, even if it's long distance. Working with a professional you trust can help you through difficult phases in nomadic life, and many counselors now do phone or web counseling.

Life Coaching: You can reach out to me for Life Coaching by contacting me on my social media pages, cosmic nomad voyager on Facebook and Instagram.

3. TIPS TO AVOID BURN OUT:

Remember your why. (See chapter one.)

Understand that this will be a process. (See chapter four, Change cycle.)

Expect a period of adjustment that might be difficult, but know this too shall pass!

If you start feeling burnt out, make rest and self-care a priority.

Do something creative. It helps to relax our nervous system and resets our brain chemistry.

Get some extra pampering, like paying for a long, hot shower. This has helped me feel better countless times.

Get help if you need it, reach out to your community.

Know it will get better!

The YouTube video, "How to mentally prepare for living in a vehicle," by Robert Witham, is an excellent source of information whether you're in the planning stage, or already on the road.

"If you get tired, learn to rest, not to quit." ~ Proctor Gallagher Institute

CHAPTER SIX: DOWNSIZING, PURGING, AND CLEARING, OH MY!

"Getting to the next level always requires ending something, leaving it behind, and moving on. Without the ability to end things, people stay stuck, never becoming who they are meant to be, never accomplishing all that their talents and abilities could afford them."
- Henry Cloud

One of the most daunting challenges we face in becoming a nomad is downsizing our precious possessions. If we've raised families and taken more than a few spins around the sun, there's significant STUFF that must go.

Some nomads call this mind-boggling process THE PURGE.

The Purge, an outwardly practical process that takes us on a fantastic inward emotional journey, is an unavoidable step towards nomadism.

While the process of the "purge" related to nomadic life may seem overwhelming, the word itself has a positive meaning: **Purge:**

1. To rid of whatever is impure or undesirable; cleanse; purify.

2. To rid, clear, or free (usually followed by of/ or from).

3. To remove by cleansing or purifying (often followed by away, off, or out).

Although it may seem intimidating, the purging of our accumulated possessions is an invaluable opportunity to cleanse and purify our lives!

One of the gifts of the Purge is that it gives us the opportunity to step into our own power ... the power to **DEFINE FOR OURSELVES WHAT IS PERSONALLY MEANINGFUL.** This process can take a while, from a few weeks to a few years, depending on where we are in our move toward nomadism, but each small step forward gets us closer to freedom. When we not just believe, but know, that *life experiences are more important to us than stuff,* we'll be propelled into more conscious, meaningful living, even if we never take the plunge into nomadic life.

When We Let Go, We Become Free!

For Capitalistic Western culture to thrive, it must convince its citizens to believe ... and more importantly to *feel* ... that physical possessions are not just optional, but *necessary* for a normal life. Just walk into any department store, grocery store or discount store, step back and with an open mind, observe the *never-ending* aisles of stuff. We're conditioned by modern media to crave this overwhelming variety of material goods ... objects we can touch, smell, see, taste, hear. The research that goes into studying exactly how we're compelled to buy these items is a multi-billion-dollar industry in itself... an industry utterly dependent on our continued consumerism.

In turn, our worth is measured by our material possessions; by the number of things we're able to accumulate.

We end up filling our homes with all the stuff we've been convinced to buy, and *having things accumulated around us* helps us to feel satisfied, safe and secure, in part an ancient biological imperative to have enough provisions stored up for hard times. *Having possessions provides a sense of security.*

Not only that, our brain chemistry also *rewards* us for shopping and buying! Shopping, whether digitally or in a physical store, triggers a flood of the "good-feeling" neurotransmitter dopamine. Dopamine is released in the brain when we encounter something new, when we're *considering* a purchase, or even just having a *craving* for more. The human brain naturally seeks novelty, which marketers understand. Our own brain chemistry is being manipulated so we'll stay motivated to *buy more stuff!*

Since dopamine is also released naturally in copious quantities when we travel and seek new sights … there's no lack in good feeling dopamine rushes living as a nomad! (****Disclaimer: I'm not an expert in neuroscience. Information on Dopamine can be found on the internet, and is only for discussion purposes in this context.)*

So why is it so hard to get rid of our STUFF???

We've been convinced that *keeping* all the stuff is reasonable *because*:

The stuff makes our lives easier.
We might need the stuff someday, tomorrow, or a far-off day in the future.
The stuff includes personally meaningful mementos.
The stuff gives us a sense of security, of having, of not lacking.
The stuff gives us a sense of control in this crazy out-of-control world.
The stuff FEELS valuable.
The stuff has sentimental value - it was Mom's Dads, Grandma's, belongs in the family, etc.

Some items we own are considered practical necessities, (let's face it indoor plumbing is awesome) while other possessions are personally meaningful only to us, symbols that evoke emotions and memories around particular experiences in our lives.

Whether our possessions fall into either the practical or sentimental, when we start downsizing it really comes down to just a few decisions about what to do with each item:

Sell it.
Give it away.
Throw it away.
Store it.
Take it with you.

A rare few are able to just walk away and leave it all behind.

There's no question that purging brings up challenging emotions. I cried many tears going through pictures of my kids! When we go through possessions tucked away in our physical closets, we're bound to uncover emotions buried in our emotional closets. We may have intense feelings over some items, finding ourselves flooded with nostalgia. Or, we may experience flashbacks of painful memories. Purging is an opportunity to sit with these emotions as they come up and finally get closure. Stay with the process. Be gentle with yourself, take breaks, get a friend to help, focus on your WHY. (From chapter one.) Remember what kind of life you crave for your future. *This is your chance to completely move on and have a fresh start!*

When I moved into my own apartment after the end of my second marriage, I bought new furniture, something I'd never been able to do for myself. It was a thrill to invest in a few pieces to furnish my cozy little apartment, and eight years later as I prepared for nomadic life, I sold or gave it all away. Cute wooden end tables, decorative plant stands, office desk and chair, filing cabinets, all the furniture I'd picked out and fell in love with - everything got sold to help finance my journey. There were some pangs of loss, but it wasn't until it came to selling my office desk that I became unexpectedly emotional. The desk was a symbol of how far I'd come in my life, of establishing my Life Coaching business, becoming an entrepreneur, and of the independence I'd worked so hard for as a single woman. When it sold, I was in tears.

I'd also kept my beautiful cedar-post bed, the first new bed I'd ever bought. I couldn't let it go, and put it in storage with some other personal items. After 10 months on the road I was ready to sell the bed and empty the storage … with surprisingly very little emotional attachment left!

By then, my rich experiences as a nomad had transcended any sadness in letting go of my past!

If we're selling our stuff, it's tempting to hold out for every last cent, but can be a rude awakening to find that our most sentimental possessions have little monetary value. One of the things I was prepared to sell was an old hand-painted Chinese vase I'd inherited, handed down from my Grandmother to my Mother … that after doing some research turned out to be worth about 30 bucks. My daughter now has it in her living room!

If holding on to *material things* is impeding our progress towards freedom, we need to reevaluate. Letting go of a potential few dollars is a small price to pay for the rich experiences waiting for us in our future!

Ask yourself whether you're going to spend your precious time trying to squeeze out every last cent from your stuff … or can you let go, even a little, and decide to spend your time on the life experiences you crave?

Besides our relationships, time and experiences are our most precious life currencies!

If we can't sell something, can we give it to someone who might appreciate it as much as we did? There are plenty of human beings in need in this world, and they aren't hard to find. Local shelters, food pantries, and social service agencies will be glad to direct you. If you feel guilty just throwing things away, make a generous contribution to humanity and pass your stuff along where you know it will be appreciated.

One of the things I had in storage was an old beat-up antique dresser that belonged to my Grandmother. I had childhood memories of seeing it in her bedroom, and it was one of the last things to go when I finally emptied the storage. I decided to give it to a furniture restorer who would refinish it, and no doubt make a few hundred bucks on it … not a small amount of money for me to pass up. Realistically, I knew I'd never have the time or motivation to do it myself, but by letting it go, I not only emptied my storage, but was also able to give Grandma's old dresser new life!

It may give us a feeling of security to hang on to our stuff, but science supports that it feels even better to give. Our brain releases dopamine and other good feeling neurotransmitters when we shop … but according to an article in psychology today, we get an even better rush of good feeling brain chemistry when we give! (Psychology Today: The Neuroscience of Giving.)

It felt a little heartless to ditch the family heirlooms, (no one else in the family wanted them) but now, as a nomad, I experience much more deeply felt emotions than when the heirlooms were tucked safely away in storage. After just over a year on the road, I'd already made cherished memories and relationships, and had experiences that I would have totally missed out on if I hadn't let go of the STUFF.

Let's face it, most heirlooms get packed away and never looked at, passed from closet to closet, forcing us to keep finding a place for them. I've kept a few small items of my Mother's, and have never regretted letting go of the rest. What I do regret are the conversations I never had with my relatives when they were alive. What were their life experiences? Who were they? What was their life story and how did they feel about it? I had Grandma's dresser, but I never really knew who she was.

If we can't sell or give away our stuff, throwing things away might feel wasteful, but once we're on the road, *we have the opportunity to become more conscious consumers and to care directly for the incredible planet that gives us life.* Boondocking in mostly free places gives me the opportunity to give back to Mother Earth. I've made a habit of picking up cigarette butts, pieces of glass and other assorted garbage other humans have left behind. Traveling across the country, I got to see first-hand how we're affecting the planet we call home, making me even more aware of the human impact on the Earth's precious and delicate eco-systems. It's unfortunate, and eye-opening, to see how little the Earth is cared for by some of its inhabitants.

We may feel guilty about being wasteful ... yet most of us regularly add to the denigration of the planet by purchasing more and more stuff over-packaged in plastic, contributing to ever enlarging piles of waste. Even with recycling, plastic waste is accumulating faster than we can get rid of it, including an island of plastic floating in the Pacific Ocean between California and Hawaii that's twice the size of Texas, and still growing. (USA Today: World's largest collection of ocean garbage is twice the size of Texas.)

Even when we know intellectually it must be done, purging and downsizing can turn into an anxious struggle for some of us. It can throw us into a state of mind called Cognitive Dissonance ... a fancy phrase that in simpler terms means we're holding two conflicting thoughts in our minds ... our own beliefs are in conflict with each other. The old thinking, *"I must hang on to all the stuff,"* - is in direct conflict with a new thought, - *"I crave the freedom of being a nomad."* The trick is to train our brains to UN-accumulate stuff, by examining the thoughts and beliefs holding us back.

Purging can bring up fear that we'll get rid of something *we might need on some unknown mystery day in the future.* Is our fear of letting go of something *we might someday possibly need* really the symptom of a deeper insecurity? Could we be trying to *soothe uncertainty over our future* by trying to predict everything we'll need ... a type of control over an unpredictable life? Security is just an illusion, whether we're in sticks and bricks or out on the road. (See chapter two on fear.)

So what happens if we do end up needing something we decided to get rid of? Ok, *So What???* So, we repurchase an item again because we need it. It doesn't sound very frugal, and yes, many of us are constrained by financial considerations, but I've never lacked for anything on the road. A common practice among the nomadic community is to give away or trade what they don't need with other nomads, and often it's synchronistic, coming along just as we need it! As YouTuber nomad Debra Dickinson says, *"The Road Provides."*

Remember as you downsize that everything you decide to keep will need a place in your vehicle. You may be able to *use* an item, but where will you put it? How much weight will it add, especially in a smaller vehicle? I had a rude awakening on my first trip when my 6 cylinder mini-van struggled to get up the steep hills of the Adirondack highways!

As a nomad, you'll learn to think about functionality in small spaces. Are there items that can be used for multiple purposes? Do you have duplicates that can be purged? If you need helpful ideas, and most of us do, there are countless articles, YouTube videos, and blogs on downsizing. Just google "how to downsize for nomadic living," or another similar phrase.

Based on my own experience, and discussions with other nomads, the downsizing process continues even when we're on the road. In my "old life" I'd collected wine glasses, rocks glasses, martini glasses and shot glasses … and was very sentimentally attached to them. Raising my two children as a single Mom there wasn't much money to splurge, so when I was finally financially secure enough to have a collection of wine glasses, it felt delicious. I finally felt like a grown up! One set was bought after a grueling divorce, symbolizing my renewed independence. Some of the wine glasses were my Mother's, passed from her Mother, which made them sentimentally important. No one in the family wanted them … and those two boxes of old wine glasses ended up getting sold for 20 bucks. A few of the newer wine glasses were distributed to my daughters, except for one martini glass, one wine glass, a few shot glasses, and a rocks glass, which I took on the road, wrapped and stored carefully for travel. In the first major purge that happened within days of my launch, they were the first things to go … except for two shot glasses which I still occasionally enjoy. Once in a while I miss making myself a drink in a "real" glass … but the pangs of missing a cocktail glass don't even come close to outweighing the life experiences I'm having on the road! The thrill of stunning vistas, of setting foot in places I'd only dreamed of, and of meeting fascinating humans, more than compensates for what I've left behind!

Another thing I purged *before and after* getting on the road was clothing, a common experience among female nomads. As a nomad I learned I could wear certain pieces of clothing more than once before they really needed to be laundered, and I purged duplicates of sweats and t-shirts, finding I could rotate through a small number of outfits. I wear my "outdoor" clothes multiple times if they're just getting a little desert dust on them, and keep my "going out" clothes separate, so I always have clean clothes for traveling or going into town. Instead of having 5 loads at the laundromat, now I have one or two. I met one female nomad who hand-washes t-shirts and small items. Another recycles outfits often, frequenting thrift shops when she gets tired of wearing the same thing. As I heard one nomad say, she waits to do laundry until her clothes are just over being too dirty! This doesn't mean nomads are filthy, this woman was clean and presentable, and hygiene is a much talked about topic among female nomads … but we've weaned ourselves off the advertising propaganda that counts on us believing that we need to spend half our lives cleaning up, or wear a different outfit every single day.

We become free finding out how little we actually need!

Having lots of possessions may give us a sense of security in an insecure world, but what do we really own? My mother wasn't a full-blown hoarder, but she got off on the dopamine rush of shopping, filling the four-bedroom home vacated by her grown kids with STUFF. Every room in her house, including a large cellar, was a depository of old stuff, new stuff, stuff she bought and stuff she never looked at again. It was a family joke at Christmas that there was always a bag of stuff somewhere that she forgot to wrap! When she developed Alzheimer's Disease and had to sell her home, *the downsizing was epic!* She insisted on keeping a good part *"the stuff"* in storage, and when she finally went into assisted living, we had to downsize again. I still have anxious dreams about the years of sorting through her stuff.

At the end of her life, the only thing that mattered was her loved ones. **Only love was real**, the relationships and connections she'd made throughout her life. The physical possessions she'd spent a lifetime filling her home with ... all the stuff of illusions that she'd determinedly held on to over the years ... had zero meaning when she was stripped down to her barest human self. It was a humbling experience.

I carry a few small mementos of my Mother, small and light enough to bring along on my journey. I know the love in my heart will always be enough to remember her by. We nomads carry our sentiments in our hearts!

My mother's passing was the beginning of a radical evolution of what was important in my own life, and purging my belongings had begun years before I was even thinking about becoming a nomad. This was influenced in a big way by being forced to deal with the mountains of my Mother's *stuff*. Little did I know, I was prepping for a journey my soul knew was coming long before my conscious mind did!

I just knew that I didn't want my STUFF to own ME. Having stuff meant I had to find a place to put it, to store it, periodically handle it, and move it. *All of that takes time and energy away from what we really want to be doing with our lives.* If I didn't get rid of it, my kids would have to deal with it later on like I did with my Mother. Having STUFF forced me to have the means to be able to keep it and care for it … by renting or owning a home, or paying for storage.

Just as our material possessions symbolize something to us, the purge is symbolic of an ending, and every ending must be fully grieved to move on. Purging almost always brings up grief as we let go of one way of life, even though we're getting ready to live an ultimately freer and more satisfying lifestyle. We may have to grieve relationships, or come to terms with how our relationships will change once we start traveling. ***Purging gives us the opportunity to finally let go of our past life-story, as we move on to create a better, more life-affirming story for ourselves.***

Sarah Seidelmann, author of the books Born to Freak, Book of Beasties, and Swimming with Elephants, wrote this beautiful piece, *"Letting Go Of Material Stuff. What To Do When Resistance Shows Up. "* In the article she describes a ritual she created to navigate her own downsizing process, saying, *"First, I take some time to say thank you for the gifts the goods have given me (steady transportation- thanks car!)* **and then**, *I say a prayer that this material thing will find its new owner who will love and appreciate it. In this way, I am a willing participant in the sacred circulation of goods/gifts. To receive, we must let go. It is the way things are. "* (Credit, Sarah Seidelmann) What an elegantly beautiful and simple way to let go!

Many objects we handle as we purge will have deep meaning to us, whether conscious or unconscious. If we're having trouble letting go of material things, we might ask, "what part of my past am I still holding on to?" What underlying meaning does this object hold for me? What do I have "stored away" in my psyche that I still haven't dealt with? What is coming up to be healed?"

If we are grieving the loss of our stuff…where have we not finished mourning some other loss in our lives? Have we come to terms with our past? If we're angry, who are we still angry with? If we're afraid, what are we afraid of and how can we make our escape from this fear-trap? If letting go of accumulated possessions makes us anxious, can we visualize living with a new sense of security, connection, and meaning without all the stuff?

Purging is an opportunity to ask ourselves, "Without material possessions, what defines me … and who do I want to be in this world?"

This purging process isn't easy, but it can be a time of letting go and closure that brings incredible personal growth. We can be free from materialism, and replace it with deeply felt emotions, community, and life experiences as a free Wild Woman On The Road.

As you go through your own purge, keep reminding yourself that you're replacing material possessions with even more precious life experiences!

During the final purge before moving out of my apartment, it helped to focus on this question: What do I want my gravestone to say? "I kept all the stuff?" Or ... *that "I'VE LIVED!?"*

"By letting go of what we've already lost we open our arms to what's trying to reach us." ~ Martha Beck

The Dig Deeper prompts for this chapter will help you get through the intimidating purge!

DIG DEEPER: TIPS TO KEEP YOUR SANITY DURING THE PURGE

"You can't declutter your living space without de-cluttering your inner life, and vice versa." - Martha Beck

The following exercise, called the **Living Space Metaphor**, is based on the idea that our external environment reflects our internal states with surprising accuracy. (Living Space Metaphor Exercise: Credit Martha Beck Inc.) As you read further, you'll learn how this exercise can help as you minimize your belongings.

Living Space Metaphor

To do the Living Space Metaphor exercise, begin by taking a mental inventory of every room in your house (or if you're already a nomad, your vehicle), taking note of your most favorite place and your least favorite place. Write down what you like or dislike about those spaces, using descriptive words of what you see in the room, and how you feel about it. For example, what you might say about your sleeping quarters: "My bedroom is messy, with clutter everywhere. It makes me feel crowded and helpless."

Now ask yourself, "How is my least favorite space like another area of dissatisfaction in my life? What area of my life feels similar to the least favorite space in my home? How can I improve my least favorite space? Using the above example, where do you feel crowded and helpless in your life? What would make you feel less crowded?

This exercise will often bring up "ah-ha" moments.

For example, maybe we have a rarely used area that gets dusty or dirty, the last room in the house to get attention, even though in the back of our minds we intend to someday get to it. We might ask ourselves, where in our inner lives do we need to clean up old painful thoughts? Do we need to clear out of a toxic relationship? Where do we need to pay more time and attention to self-care?

If we've got lots of clutter, what do we need to cut out of our lives that isn't contributing to our well-being? What weighs us down and makes us feel heavy with responsibility or sadness?

Conversely, contemplate a favorite area of our living space, and notice the feelings that come up. Ask, how does this give me pleasure? What feelings do I get from this space, for example, light, airy, competent? How does this space provide me with joy and happiness? Where do I have this same feeling in my life?

Using the living space metaphor as a jumping off point, we can modify this exercise to include the objects we're trying to purge.

If strong emotions bubble up over an object as you purge, ask yourself what area of your life you're reminded of as you handle this object. Is it financial? Personal? Relationships? Family? Career? Are there issues in those areas that haven't been resolved?

Use the Living Space Metaphor to discover the emotional baggage connected to items in your downsizing project.

What does the item remind you of?

What are you making that mean?

In what areas of your life are you having trouble letting go?

Journal what comes up!

Use your Body Compass to decide how and what to purge.

Go back to chapter three and review your Body Compass. The Dig Deeper exercises for that chapter will guide you to your own Body Compass, the internal guidance system that tells us the truth.

For the items you're struggling to purge, hold or touch the item, and tune in to your Body Compass, asking these questions one at a time:

Do I sell this item?
Do I give it away?
Do I store this item?
Do I throw it away?
Do I bring this item on my journey?

If your Body Compass is calibrated as discussed in Chapter three, you'll get sensations that give you yes or no answers. If there's no clear answer, set the item aside and come back to it later.

There are also plenty of techniques for downsizing that can be searched on the internet, like Marie Kondo.

Answer this question: Once you've purged, what do you need to *ADD TO YOUR LIFE* that brings joy?

This could be crafts or other hobbies you bring on the road. For example, I brought books that were dear to me, a small container with beading supplies, my hemp jewelry making supplies, crystals, and my guitar.

You will get through the purge, and when you're done, you'll feel freer and lighter than ever!

*"Freedom is available at anytime, to anyone
- and so is captivity."*
~ Martha Beck, in her book, Steering By Starlight

ADDENDUM: INVENTORY IN MY VAN

I've included this information to give you an idea of what can fit in a mini-van, and what I've purged over the years.

This is by no means a final list; every few months items still get switched out and purged! If I haven't touched or worn something in 6 months, and it's not a seasonal item, I consider purging it.

I'm not a minimalist in the strictest sense, but fitting everything you own into a mini-van is by its very nature a minimalist venture. That being said, it is surprising what you can fit into small spaces!

The inside of my van has all back seats removed, and the usable floor space the back of the van is about 4' x 8'.

Some items only go in the van when I travel, like chairs and tables.

IN FRONT OF VAN:

8 gallons of water in refillable one-gallon jugs. Stored on front floor passenger side.
Water filter on front passenger seat.

2 Gallon water container on front passenger seat.
Maps in the passenger side door pocket.
Hung over front seat backs: Flannels. Hoodies. Rain coat.
Button up shirt.

Stored throughout the Van In Small Spaces:

Assorted tarps
Shade cloths
Small 12V Fan
Battery Operated fan
Jumper cables
Mosquito netting.
Heavy duty extension cord. Extension cord with power
strip.
Backpack
Hammock
Small indoor/outdoor rug.
Tent poles for awning.
Lightweight puffer jacket.
2 Solar panels
2 batteries
Porta-potti

I've purged since first starting out: Battery jump starter
with cables. I've downsized to a handheld battery jump
starter.
Sine wave converter. - PURGED

UNDER THE BED:

I found it interesting to go through this list years later and see what I've purged! I left some of it in the list with the word "purged" after the items I no longer have.

3 Bins containing:

One bin of clothes. Includes all warm and cool weather clothes, bandanas, T-shirts, long sleeve shirts, tank-tops. Two pairs of jeans - one for outdoor wear, one for "going to town." Three pairs of yoga pants. Two pairs of sweats. Two pairs of shorts. Two lightweight hoodies.

Winter gloves – PURGED.
Two winter coats. – PURGED.
Ponchos. - PURGED
One pair of black dress boots (never worn yet but I'm keeping just in case -nope, PURGED!)
Mud boots - PURGED.
Assorted paperwork, books.

Stored in open plastic bins for easy access:
Three pairs of sneakers, one pair of flip-flops, hiking boots. One heavy sweatshirt and one thick sweater.

Battery operated shower. - PURGED
Small soft-sided lunch box cooler - PURGED

Collapsible water bucket – PURGED.
Air mattress pump – PURGED.

Stored in the very back of the van:
Coleman Classic two burner stove and one burner butane stove …. not minimalistic but I haven't yet regretted having two stoves.

Near the bed:

Laundry bag.
Shower bag with shampoo/soap/clean towel.
Soft-sided suitcase for travel. – PURGED.

Small bin with books.

Rectangular wicker basket that stores varying things like extra sweaters, socks, underwear.

Basket with essential oils, meds, nail clippers. 2 Jackknives, one carpet knife with razor blade. Portable sewing kit.

Basket with hygiene items: toothbrush/ mouthwash etc., sunscreen, bug spray, scissors, q-tips, wipes, essential oil spray, mirror, instant hot packs, Toilet paper, etc.

Hung on hooks:
Hats. Bandanas. Binoculars. Knife. Earphones. Phone charging cord.

4 sets of scissors placed in various convenient places…
one of my quirks …. you can never have too many scissors
handy on the road.

Multiple scarves.

MISC.

Bungie stretched between seat belt holders (in back of van
on side next to windows) hung with cargo netting that
holds clothes, scarves, etc.

Small collapsible stool.
Reflectix for windows
Two folding chairs. One other small portable folding chair.
Laptop/phone/charging cords.
Hot water bottle.
LOTS of blankets!
My guitar.
Miscellaneous like extra glasses, paperwork, receipts.
Crystals and rocks I've collected for over 30 years. – most
have been PURGED.
Foam pad to kneel on. - PURGED
20 Gallon Coleman Cooler. -PURGED. Now have a small
fridge running off the Jackery 500W battery.
1 umbrella.
2 foam coolers. - PURGED

One small plastic container with cleaning supplies: Rubber
gloves, cleaning clothes, scrubbies.
Spray bottles: Rinse water. Alcohol spray. Sprayer with
dish soap/water.

I have multiple sources of light in the van.
One flashlight
Little battery-operated closet lights, - PURGED.
Coleman lantern – PURGED.
One of the things I did purge was a big utility light …. one of the things I wished I'd kept! There is no perfect formula for this process!

I digitalized photos and music to store on my computer and pay a dollar a month to have it backed up. I made sure I was getting paper statements and set up online bill pay to cut down on what paperwork I'd have to handle on the road.

In two large plastic storage drawers accessed from the back is everything you'd find in your kitchen drawers, garage, or cellar. You can see my current set up on my website Cosmicnomadvoyager.com, My No Build Van Build blog.

All kitchen food items. Oil. Spices etc.
Cooking/kitchen items.
A few forks, spoons and knives and some plastic (I've subtracted and added eating utensils)
One coffee cup
Two thermoses, one for hot, one for cold- PURGED.
One thermos for coffee in the morning.
One metal mixing bowl
One cereal bowl
Spatula
Paper plates
Bullet mini blender that runs off the portable battery
Small plastic cutting boards

3 Cutting knives
Vegetable peeler
Set of camping pots, one small, one medium
One frying pan
Tongs, mixing spoon, potato masher, plastic ladle.
Small bag of basic tools.
Extra napkins, paper towels. Masking tape. Clear tape.
Utility gloves. First aid kit. Duct tape. Glue. Velcro. Bug
spray. Ropes, bungies, clothespins, tent stakes etc. Extra
work gloves. Safety glasses. Hatchet. Small foldable saw.
Hair clippers. Craft items: hemp cord, beads, beading
tools. Notebooks/Journals. Two small soft-sided jewelry
carriers with necklaces, bracelets, earrings, jewelry I've
made. Laundry detergent. Extra washcloths. Extra rags.

Two small plastic tables
One bigger folding table
All tables fold down and go in back of van for travel.

Yoga mat
Picnic blanket
2 twin air mattresses - PURGED
Coleman Telescoping camping table - PURGED
Beach shelter - PURGED
Walking Sticks
Small tent
screen shelter - PURGED

CHAPTER SEVEN: NOMADISM - A WOMEN'S MOVEMENT

"The doors to the world of the wild Self are few but precious. If you have a deep scar, that is a door, if you have an old, old story, that is a door. If you love the sky and the water so much you almost cannot bear it, that is a door. If you yearn for a deeper life, a full life, a sane life, that is a door." ~ Clarissa Pinkola Estes

I'm intrigued why we, as women, are turning in droves to nomadic life. There is, of course, the element of necessity, the brutal financial reality that over a lifetime of employment we've probably earned less than most men, had career opportunities affected by caregiving, and with modern economics and divorce, have little savings to fall back on. Despite all that, we seem to be awakening to the realization that *we don't have to settle for a life of subsidized stagnation!*

Nomadism is a growing movement. As a species, we're realizing how soul-crushing a "normal" life is, but nomadism is also a modern *women's movement.* We've been expected to be amenable participants in a society that *still* doesn't grant us sovereignty over our own choices, including choices involving sexuality and our own bodies. Since writing this book the fight for sovereignty over our choices has only gotten more intense, but with the upsurge of women nomads, we're claiming our independence! Starting with the women's lib movement back in the 60's, we've made substantial gains. (We've come a long way baby!) I believe the current influx of women into nomadic life comes from an even deeper place in our collective female psyche. As half of the human population, we're still struggling to gain sovereignty over our reproductive choices, get equal treatment as wage earners, and smash distorted expectations about our looks, (google: fat-shaming or ageism) but as nomads we're reclaiming our sovereignty as *free women* … claiming sovereignty not just over our bodies, but our minds and souls.

The sacred feminine isn't a dainty, well groomed, accommodating creature … but is a fierce, free and strong soul, one of the tribe of Women Who Run With The Wolves, as author Clarissa Pinkola Estes describes.

As modern women in the Western world, we've been born into a time when societal conditions are beneficial to our growth, and if we're lucky, we have the opportunity to experience the *freedom of self-actualization.* Compared to our sisters born as little as a hundred years ago, our way of life has drastically improved. My Grandmother was alive when women still didn't have the right to vote. Up into the late 1800's, just a few generations before us, a woman didn't have rights to her own property, or even to her own children, and was little more than an indentured servant in her own home … all without the modern household conveniences that we now take for granted. Modern, reliable methods of birth control finally set women free from the horrors of multiple births that kept them chained to the home, often ultimately claiming their lives, but it wasn't until *1960 that the FDA approved the first oral contraceptive.* After that, it wasn't until 1965, five more years, *before a married woman could legally use birth control!* And as far as financial freedom, a woman couldn't get a credit card without her husband's signature until 1974! Not to invalidate the very real struggle women still face, but now for most of us, our basic needs can be met.

There's been no better time for us to claim our personal freedom!

Nomadic life offers women a chance to expand our mind and experiences, and with a good majority of us done with parenting and caregiving, we're feeling the call to find a fulfilling life that extends beyond our grandmotherly roles as built-in babysitters and cookie makers. Not that being a cookie-making grandma can't be rewarding, I LOVED living close to my grown kids and grandkids, and becoming a remote grandma was one of the hardest things I've ever done … but we sense there is MORE for us.

Women in the nomadic tribe want something different for themselves. We're ready to be completely free, heart and soul. We want to be real. We want to be seen for who we are. We want to start living as the capable, ingenious creatures we know ourselves to be.

Outdated cultural and social rules traditionally put women in a passive role, a role that demanded we sacrifice our personal needs to satisfy the needs of everyone else around us, and it can be tempting to buy into this role, identifying with the thought, "I can't leave, everybody needs me!" When a woman chooses to drop this passive role, she claims the *freedom to be the active creative director of her own life.*

Our desire to be nomadic isn't as eccentric as some would have us believe. Not so far back in our genetic history we were natural nomads, moving when the climate changed or local resources became scarce, and no doubt it was the women around the hearth, the mothers and grandmothers, the gatherers and the wise women innately connected to Mother Earth, who knew when moving on was essential to the tribe's survival. It makes me wonder if women entering nomadic life in modern times are feeling a similar innate pressure to be mobile, in part an unconscious desire to flee from the life-negating powers that be. Listening to our inner wise woman, we're now heading out *en masse* into life-affirming nomadic journeys.

Even with improved living conditions, many women feel trapped in jobs they hate, tolerate abusive or painful relationships, and often suppress their own needs and desires until the bitter end of their lives. We may "have it all," but we're still struggling with a vague, or maybe not so vague, uneasiness that we're missing something in our lives.

Maybe our modern urge to embrace nomadic life is in reality an ancient response, an awakening of old survival mechanisms that kept our species alive. Like our hunter-gatherer ancestors who moved on in response to diminishing resources or drastic climate change, we're taking to the road in response to the media's incessant newsfeed of increasingly disturbing domestic and worldwide conflicts. Is our urge to get mobile a response not just to our own personal suffering, but to the suffering in the world that threatens to emotionally overcome us?

It makes sense that women may be outnumbering men in this call to nomadism and nature. Our women's intuition beckons us to get closer to the natural cycles of the Earth, and while the Earth struggles with the effects of human occupation, some of us are awakening to the reality that she's a living entity, struggling under the unsustainable practices damaging the environment. By answering this freedom-call to nomadism, we have the opportunity to share powerful healing energy with Mother Earth. *Living as nomads, we become immersed in nature, not as occasional outside observers or tourists, but as engaged participants in the natural world.*

On a purely practical note, it might be argued that as travelers we're consuming more fossil fuels than the average stationary dweller, but as nomads, we actually use *fewer* resources, more efficiently. By some estimates, we use about 1% - 10% of the water consumption of a traditional home. (The USGS Water Science School: How much water does the average person use at home per day?) Living in tiny spaces requires we practice less unnecessary consumerism ... there's just no place for extra items that don't serve a useful purpose ... and by default, we're adding less than the average consumer to the vast waste piles of plastic packaging. Nomads are adept in economical food storage and preparation, with less ensuing waste. Reduced consumerism means a concurrent reduction of our carbon footprint as it relates to the transportation of goods by land, sea or air, not to mention lowering the human cost of imported goods made by human beings in other countries working in appalling conditions.

What About Freedom?

Freedom is a thought-provoking concept, and one thrown around frequently by the nomadic community. If there was a study of reasons we become nomads, I bet freedom would be at the top of the list, but *how do you define freedom?*

Being out on the road I still need my Social Security check every month, medical insurance, mail delivery, internet, and other necessities. If I want to keep those benefits, I'm not free from having to deal with all the organizations that administer those services.

When I relocated to the Southwest, I wasn't free from bureaucracy, in fact, I was steeped in it for over 6 mind-numbing weeks. All the applications, phone calls, paperwork ... all the little things that had to be done to satisfy the unending checkboxes necessary to relocate from one state to another was a freedom-stealing, soul-sucking endeavor. I dealt with humans stuck in jobs they hate, providing services to people they don't really give a sh*t about ... and at times I was brought to tears. I was given inconsistent information that changed from hour to hour as I was dispatched from one department to another. I encountered what I believe was discrimination when my partner and I were refused a P.O box, after having no problems in other towns *within the same state.*

It was a rude awakening to find that requirements just for surrendering license plates differ from state to state, and the tangle of motor vehicle bureaucracy that would keep me legal in both states seemed to require a Ph.D. and the flexibility of a contortionist. I gave up hours of my life in uncomfortable, crowded waiting rooms, or on long holds and confusing conversations with multiple agencies.

I also wasn't free when I stealth parked in an area *I knew for a fact* wasn't illegal …and at 7:30 in the morning got the dreaded knock. My partner and I were given a questionably legal warning by local authorities, even though we were *well informed after checking local city codes that it wasn't illegal to sleep in a vehicle overnight in that location.* A local contact informed us that the area we'd been stealth parking in for 3 weeks had just exploded into a hotbed of debate involving nomads, locals, and authorities, which seems to be a growing problem for nomads. Although there was no specific state, town or county code that made us illegal, when the local police show up and ask you to move on, you move. My freedom to stay where I chose ended at that moment. Once again, life came along and changed our plans for us. Scrambling to adjust our resources, we accepted help from a fellow nomad to stay at a paid campground for the next few days. Our tidy plan to travel to our next destination when we got paid at the end of the week was suddenly out the window.

Unfortunately, as nomads, we're defined as homeless by most authorities, and the current political and social climate is not friendly towards us. A recent sweep of homeless encampments in Lake Elsinore, CA, resulted in 53 arrests, 41 of those for trespassing. The mayor of the town issued a press statement emphasizing that there would be zero tolerance moving forward, and promised there would be ongoing arrests of the homeless with any "material" confiscated, meaning personal possessions, and any pets involved separated from their owners and moved to shelters. 54 were offered help through a local social service agency, which over half refused. While we don't consider ourselves homeless, it's worth paying attention to these events and making sure we aren't in an area where we're at risk for this type of authoritarian intervention.

Another issue is having the freedom to access services that are widely available to citizens of the US, such as a P.O. box or necessary social services. Not having a physical structure to call a residence can sometimes be complicated on the road.

Women on the road also must also take into consideration the freedom to move about safely. While statistically we're safer out in more wild areas, we're still not entirely free from the threat of predation, either physically or emotionally. Thankfully, as the women's movement of nomadism gets more organized, and we band together sharing knowledge and support, the empowerment we gain drastically reduces our risk of becoming victims to a predator.

FREEDOM IS RELATIVE.

With all that said, and I think I speak for most nomadic women ... *I FEEL FREE!*

I've claimed personal freedom to define my life according to what makes me feel the happiest, fulfilled, and whole.

We feel the freest when we're living from our essential self, and as opposed to being selfish, a woman living as her essential self can't help but make a beneficial contribution to the larger world around her.

Forge Your Own Path.

When I first starting researching the nomadic life, I watched every video I could find that featured women on the road, studied every van build known to exist on the internet, and when I finally got on the road and started meeting other nomadic women, wanted to peek into every rig! It gave me some great ideas, but I ended up comparing my van build to sometimes impossible standards. As Martha Beck Life Coaches say, "Compare and Despair!"

I know now that what matters is that *I'M OUT THERE.* I'm living it and loving it! The *how* doesn't matter … what matters is that I'm living the life of my dreams. I've met women traveling in the Mercedes of van builds, and women who just throw in a cot and supplies and just go.

I've been able to encourage other women and have even been interviewed about nomad life and my van set up a few times. You can find those interviews on TheGalavan on YouTube.

IT ALL WORKS! What works for one person may not work for you, but it's possible to live the nomadic life within your own personal means. Don't force yourself into someone else's idea of what your vehicle should look like, where you should be traveling, or what you should be doing with your time.

159

Our personal nomadic journey will be shaped by many factors, including financial means. Gas expenses determine how far we travel, whether we pay for campsites, or boondock on free land. Our age, physical abilities, disabilities, or health issues also impact our activities. We'll discover our personal preferences: solo travel or caravanning, climate preferences, group or solo camping. Our vehicle choice will determine whether we can stealth camp or boondock, and how much we'll need to invest in maintenance.

My personal needs include shade and moderate temps, and connection with my tribe. My preferences include having a cell signal, (isolation off the grid just isn't my deal), and a good degree of privacy.

All said and done, the nomad journey is ours to make **unapologetically our own.** The nomad experience is a continual evolution of what works and what doesn't, but once we find our groove, we're on our way to creating everything we desire as a nomad, whether it be freedom, escape, healing, or living close to nature.

By creating our own way of life, we claim our right to our own space and time, the right to do what we love, and the right to determine how we use our personal energy.

Even in these modern times, we're still conditioned as women in how to think and behave. We're taught to put on the "social self" mask that's expected of us, but where does that leave us? If we let our social-self run the show, how does that limit our individual freedom, happiness, autonomy, and ultimately, our contribution to the larger world? We face a tough internal argument between our social self and essential self when we've been conditioned to believe that staying in traditional roles as women, staying put and taking care of everyone else, *is the right thing to do*.

How does that internal argument between our social self and essential-self affect us? The call of our essential self may manifest in subtle or not so subtle feelings that tell us something just isn't right in our lives. Ignoring our essential self may show up as physical or emotional distress, or as that quiet voice in the middle of the night that says change is on the way. We can continue to ignore that voice, but usually to our detriment.

When we connect with our authentic, essential beings, we're plugged into our power. We are plugged into our own Life Force, which doesn't allow us to be victimized or oppressed.

Reinvention of Your SELF

Becoming a nomad, you'll redefine what's important to you, and what it's worth to live your personal version of freedom. *As you reinvent yourself, you'll find yourself ... this is the very heart of the nomadic women's movement.*

One thing I've learned in my nomadic journey is that becoming a Wild Woman Nomad is a process, not an event, and one that starts well before we hit the road. Finally launching is a huge thrill, and one I remember vividly. My launch day felt like the culmination of all the hopes and dreams I'd had for years, *but that was just the beginning.*

There are a thousand little adjustments in becoming a *nomadic free spirit,* with changes happening on deep levels as we move through those adjustments. There's an essential re-wiring of our brain and body when we go from a sheltered stationary existence to living out in the world as a nomad, and this radical process isn't without discomfort. The trick is to know it's all ok, it's all normal, and to try to roll with the changes!

Living as a nomad changes us on a cellular level. Living in a house, before we go out we check the weather to see if we need an umbrella, but as a nomad, the weather outside is our home! There are myriads of fluctuations in temperature, air pressure, changes in sunlight, humidity, rain, clouds, and wind throughout our day as a nomad. Changes in weather, from the most severe to the most pleasant, have a direct effect on our body. We get to experience all of it, from sunrise to sunset, from the passing of the stars to the phases of the moon. As nomads we benefit immensely from fresh air, sunlight and exposure to natural spaces, with fewer EMFs, off-gassing, indoor pollution and screen time. (EMFs.World Health Organization: What are electromagnetic fields?) The modern human body, living in the industrialized, digitalized world, has lost its natural intelligence. *Our bodies have to re-learn how to be a human being living outdoors!*

Living as nomads, our bodies will learn to adapt more readily to temperature changes, our sleep patterns will

 change, hopefully for the better as we're exposed to more natural light cycles. As our metabolism changes to keep up with increased physical activity and constant adjustments to the microclimate, we'll burn more calories! (Microclimate: the climate of a small area.) If you're like me, for the first time in your life you'll experience effortless weight loss!

Our path to reinvention starts internally, and our body follows. One year, when I got back to the hot, dry Sonoran desert after camping in the Sequoia National Forest and spending time on the Pacific coast during the summer, I was pleasantly surprised that the higher temps and the blazing sun were much more bearable than when I'd first arrived in Arizona from NY state. My body had heightened its outside weather intelligence!

Living as a nomad is challenging, filled with constant change and uncertainty, and navigating life on the road is an art form. Plans frequently fall through - the campground is unexpectedly closed, travel schedules get screwed up, a crazy neighbor forces you to leave a perfect spot, you get an early morning knock from the authorities in an area previously friendly to overnight parking, the weather suddenly changes and there's a downpour before you get set up (or sandstorm or windstorm or hailstorm) things break, the weather is too hot or too cold, there are *ALL THE THINGS* that have to be done to maintain your lifestyle even though you are completely exhausted and you end up uncomfortable and questioning your life choices and there's just nothing you can f*cking do in the moment to make it better and you just say f*ck it and have a drink. I may have.

Within a few months of getting to Arizona after my trip across the US, my van's side sliding door jammed open ... which coincidentally happened right before a major dust storm on the desert. After some help from friendly nomads in removing the fuse, I bungeed the door closed, stuffed towels in the cracks and made it through the storm ... of course followed by an expensive repair that made a mess of my finances. The same month, new and acute back pain sent me to a local emergency room. This all happened as a solo female nomad, with no partner for support and my entire family 3,000 miles away across the continent. Nomadic life can be less stressful than traditional living, but it sometimes hits you with its own flavor of stress. Be forewarned, this lifestyle demands its price in emotional resiliency. For many women, this is the first time in their lives they're out on their own and not dependent on someone else, a perfect opportunity to discover their inner Wild Woman and how fierce and strong they really are. When people tell me they're jealous of my lifestyle, I just can't help myself ... I have to laugh. There are times when I am absolutely miserable as a van-dwelling nomad.

Then ... there comes the rush of absolute freedom and joy on the road, of seeing the world as you've never seen it, of standing on an ocean beach far from your home of origin, with frothy waves rolling over your feet and the sun and sky and cries of seagulls filling your senses, of having your mind blown as you look down from a high mountain peak on a psychedelic orange sunset, of meeting fellow nomads

164

who inspire and challenge you to make your nomadic life even better, and give you the encouragement and support that comes just the right moment. Or, like me, you start out as a solo female van dweller and meet the love of your life on the desert …and event so delicious and surprising that would never have happened had I not taken the leap of faith to become a nomad!

There will be stress on the road, but we can control how we frame our experiences. If we have a habit of always focusing on the negative before we get on the road, we'll experience the same negativity as a nomad. No matter where we are in life, sh*t happens, as they say, but if we can get a handle on the effort and resiliency needed to be nomads, we'll revel in the physical, mental, emotional and spiritual benefits. Personally, *any stress I experience as a nomad is without a doubt worth the wonder of the life I live.*

Find Your Community.

When I started my nomadic journey, I thought I was seeking solitude, but quickly learned how much I need human connection as a nomad.

As a confirmed introvert who'd lived happily alone for many years, I was surprised that I was lonely on the road, and the antidote was to strike up conversations with just about anyone, including forest rangers and store clerks. I discovered a friendly extroverted part of myself that I never knew existed! Once I got to the Southwest, where multitudes of nomads roam, I started making in-person connections with women and men who've now become part of my growing tribe.

You'll find that nomadic life attracts all kinds of humans living outside of the mainstream, a vast variety of people who refuse to fit into the boxes society would prefer they stay. I've met a few storytellers along the way, like the man struggling to keep his stories straight, claiming he was a multi-millionaire but later slipping up when he mentioned his budget wouldn't allow a 72 dollar park entrance fee ... another camper found my partner and me to be a captive audience to his tales of lunches with Carol Burnett, his years working as a sound system tech for Barry White, and who after helping the authorities clean up the scene of a murder, had his vehicle and trailer molotov cocktailed in Slab City! Nancy and I now have *our story* prepared for the next teller of tall tales ... we were the inspiration for Tina Turner's hit song, Private Dancer ... we're two retired lap dancers, Pepper and Sugar, and after we ran a successful con on our high-level handlers, we took to the road ... and we've been on the run for 40 years! Do you think anyone would believe us? LOL!

As a nomad, you'll meet people with a wide variety of world-views and temperaments, interesting humans who've broken out of the mold. With time, you'll also learn which humans to invite into your private circle, and who to avoid.

When I first started meeting other nomadic women, I'd give out my phone number right away and make myself available to anyone who seemed in need. That's what we're supposed to do, right? Support our sisters? While I'm pretty good with my Body Compass (see chapter 3), I have trouble reading people. After having some emotionally draining interactions, I learned that having personal boundaries is essential in protecting my own energy and well-being. That doesn't mean we don't support other women, but there's a difference between taking care of someone with a habit of dependency and giving support to an independent female nomad in need.

For the most part, women on the road are seeking empowerment, which is peaceful, cooperative and tolerant. I've also come across world-views that are so incompatible with mine that there's no common ground that feels safe. My partner and I met some seemingly friendly nomads and were invited to their potluck, which we attended as an obviously lesbian couple. Days later we were informed by one of the attendees that some ugly comments about our sexual preferences occurred after we left. While I understand we heard this second hand, it spoke to the general climate of the group. C'est La Vie. Not everyone you meet will end up being part of your tribe.

Led by our inner vision, our inward journey is one we take alone, but that vision connects us all as a tribe!

Despite the news feeds and media portrayal to the contrary, people are generally good, and most nomads are willing to help out a fellow nomad in need, even if it's just company and a meal. If you're lonely on the road, *look for your tribe!* Be open to talking to other nomads. Make eye contact, wave, say hello ... most people will give you a signal that they're open to socializing, or not.

Respect camp "homesteads" by not entering the outer boundaries unless you get a clear invitation. Keep in mind, as nomads we need to practice a higher level of courtesy and tolerance living outside together. A friendly "hello, anyone home," or "do you mind some company" from a reasonable distance is an acceptable way to approach someone from outside their living area. On that note, my partner and I met on the Arizona desert when she walked by my van and noticed my (then) New York state license plates, coincidentally also her home state ... she started up a conversation and the rest, as they say, is history!

Our growing tribe of nomadic women is always there to help you on your way. At the beginning of my journey, I met several nomadic women willing to take me under their wing as a newbie, taking time and energy out of their own journey to mentor me. We, as Wild Women On The Road, are indeed warriors on the front lines of this growing women's movement, deeply invested in the well-being and success of each of us in this beautiful tribe!

"The only way to deal with an unfree world is to become so absolutely free that your very existence is an act of rebellion." ~ Albert Camus

Read on to DIG DEEPER and explore your personal women's movement.

DIG DEEPER: EXPLORING YOUR PERSONAL WOMEN'S MOVEMENT

"You really can only build a happy life on the foundation of your own nature." ~ Gretchen Rubin - The Happiness Project

The following questions will help you explore your inner journey and get clearer on your personal truth.

Give yourself time for self-reflection. Journal. Seek solitude. Find a way to listen to that inner voice that says *there's got to be something more to your life.*

If you don't know where to start, find a life coach or therapist that can help.

Questions for Self-Exploration

1. What is an individual area of discomfort that might be a message from your essential self? (i.e., guilt, unhappiness, worry, physical illness, emotional distress, dreams) Like the Body Compass you learned about in Chapter three, the body is always speaking to us.

To hear the profound messages from your body, the ego-mind must first be quieted. Start by using breathing exercises, meditation, or relaxation exercises to first still your mind.

When you feel sufficiently relaxed, move your attention to a place in your body that you feel needs attention.

For a moment, suspend logical belief, and ask the following questions. After each question, listen internally for an answer. You may get a visual in your mind, have an idea bubble up, or just have an intuition about what's going on.

What is my body attempting to convey?

Is there a message from my body right now?

What does that message mean to you?

When you're done, consciously thank your body for the messages and its miraculous functions.

Be sure to journal what comes up. Even if it doesn't make sense right now, chances are it will in the future.

2. If you're feeling guilty: The minute you feel any guilt, send love to it, stop, and listen to its message. That message is from your inner self, asking permission to love yourself.

What do you feel guilty about? Why?

Use the above statement to explore a possible polar opposite to your guilt. Often guilt is a smokescreen coming from the ego that's trying to prevent us from living our dreams.

Answer this: If guilt miraculously disappeared from your emotional landscape, what would you go out and do right now that would bring you satisfaction, pleasure, and fulfillment? (Without harming another person.)

3. What is the predominant feeling you're looking for as a nomad? Is there more than one way to achieve that feeling?

For example, when I first started researching nomadic life, I was looking for a Class C RV, and I ended up with a mini-van. I've still fulfilled my dream of ***nomadic freedom*** on the road, but it looks completely different from my initial vision.

Journal about the predominant feeling, or reason, that you're drawn to nomadic life. Without censoring or having to know how or why, describe three different ways that could become a reality for you.

4. What thoughts run through your mind that discourage you from becoming a nomad?

Can you know for sure that those thoughts are in your best interest?

The Work, a powerful technique for healing founded by Byron Katie, asks four simple questions designed to set us free from suffering. You can find instructions and information on how to do The Work with your own painful thoughts on her website, The Work Of Byron Katie. http://thework.com/en/do-work.

Are the reasons you can't get on the road *your* reasons, or do you hear reasons in your head that "everybody else" has for you? We all have a voice that's a conglomerate of what we *THINK* people are saying about us. When we actually try to name who is saying what, we may find that the "everybody voice" may be coming from our imagination! (See chapter 2 on fear, and chapter 3 on Body Compass.)

Review the body compass chart (North Star O-Meter) from chapter 3 and explore your discouraging thoughts while checking in with your body compass. What negative or positive effects do these thoughts have on your well-being, and your future plans?

5. Do you have a reoccurring vision that inspires you to become a nomad? Make a vision board! Start by browsing magazines and pull out the images, words or phrases that move you. Don't think about it too much, just let your heart and intuition be your guide. Cut out the images and glue them onto poster board any way you like. This isn't just woo-woo, making a vision board can help us create the life we desire: *The Reason Vision Boards Work and How To Make One.* (Huffington Post: The Reason Vision Boards Work And How To Make One.)

7. Ask yourself these Large Questions: (attributed to Michele Woodward, Life Coach)

1. Who am I apart from the roles I play?

2. Does the path I'm on enlarge or diminish me?

3. What do I want my life to mean?

172

"Take your life in your own hands, and what happens? A terrible thing: no one to blame." ~ Erica Jong

CHAPTER EIGHT: NOW FOR A BIT OF THE PRACTICAL STUFF

"Start by doing what's necessary; then do what's possible; and suddenly you are doing the impossible." ~ Saint Francis of Assisi

Today is errand day. On my to-do list: fill up the gas tank, bring out the garbage, check on butane supplies for the stove, which is getting eaten up like crazy due to the wind, take care of my human waste. Rain is in the forecast, and before leaving camp, I move a few things around so they don't get soaked. My first stop in town is Auto Zone to look for a replacement fuse for my portable battery which is suddenly not charging, (Uggghhhh!) followed by the library to continue to write my heart and soul out to you. My partner is out on the town today too, getting her car looked at for a possible electrical problem, (which we spent half the day yesterday troubleshooting) and she'll be filling up the water jugs and getting us an easy dinner for us to enjoy at the end of "maintenance" day. The cooler will need ice in a few days, grocery shopping needs to be done, along with the never-ending maintenance and organization it takes to thrive in a small living space ... or be at risk for losing one's sanity! That doesn't include the cooking and cleaning up that takes twice as long without running water and a dishwasher!

Even writing this book has taken conscious planning. With no electrical outlet to conveniently charge up my laptop, and currently no solar, I either run the van engine and charge it off a small 12v sine converter, or take a trip to the town library. (Since then I've invested in solar.)

The practical aspects of this life are abundant!

Because this book isn't meant as a practical guide, you won't find detailed instructions for nomadic living in this chapter, but hopefully the more general, philosophical information that can guide you in making your own practical decisions. You'll find an abundance of resources for practical guidance in the resources list at the end of this book, and because the nomadic world is expanding exponentially, you can pretty much google any question you have about nomadic life and find the answer.

Living comfortably as a nomad takes organization, a solid routine, and the physical and emotional resilience to pull it all off.

Peeing and pooping, eating and sleeping, sex and housekeeping still happen the same as in a traditional stick and brick dwelling, *but we nomads are geniuses at pulling it off on the road!*

Instead of paying a utility company an extortionist's price for the privilege of staying warm in the cold Northeastern winters, out in the Southwest I follow the sun, run the car heater before bed, heat up water for my hot water bottle, and have lots of blankets. This is part of my freedom, and what a happy dance I did (and possibly some middle finger gesturing) paying the last bill to the utility company! With practice and acclimation, a 40-degree night now feels comfortable in my mini-van, something I would never have tolerated back in my sheltered apartment days.

We pay the price of freedom on the road by meeting our needs in a more hands-on way, which shapes the quality of our lives as nomads. I can't just flick a switch and hope to pay the utility bill once a month to have lights and heat, or flush my bodily waste down the toilet without having to think about it, look at it, or handle it. The smallest tasks, including hygiene, take constant planning … most nomads have become experts with spray bottles and pumps, outdoor showers, and water conservation. A real shower with running hot and cold water is a luxury much looked forward to in a nomad's world!

If we measure our lives by modern conveniences, the life of a nomad appears to have moved backward in time, but in reality, *we've moved forward in living an authentic life and experiencing the world firsthand.* For me, going back to a comfortable yet sheltered life in a stick and brick home feels like a terrifying move backward!

So how do we get our needs met as Wild Women On The Road?

When it comes to what we physically need, the human basics are just a few, as we can see with this list loosely based on Maslow's Hierarchy of Basic Needs.

Our physical needs are:

Shelter from the elements.

Air.

Water.

Food.

Waste disposal: Catching, storage, and disposal of human waste and other refuse.

Hygiene.

Temperature control.

Bed/Sleep.

Clothing.

Sex.

Physical movement.

Safety.

(I'd add ease of access to medical care and essential services.)

According to Maslow's theory, once our basic physical needs are met, we can move on to filling our emotional needs, which vary in importance according to our individual temperaments:

Companionship.

Community.

Love, including self-love.

Safety. (also a physical need)

Affection.

Belonging.

Intimacy. (not sex)

Confidence.

Achievement.

Independence.

Freedom.

Self-respect and respect from others. (Self-esteem)

Spirituality if individually applicable.

Peace.

Happiness.

Following Maslow's theory, once our physical, social, emotional and spiritual needs are met, we're free to explore the more esoteric personal meaning of our lives. We may discover a deep need for self-fulfillment, and in this state of self-actualization we find a natural progression to becoming more altruistic, wishing for the wellbeing of not just ourselves, but for humanity as a whole. *As nomads, we often encounter the attitude that we're just*

***bums living on the road, but in fact, many of us have an
acute awareness of our contribution to humanity as a
whole.***

While we may be on the road in a quest for higher
meaning, our basic physical needs come first, with one of
our most practical needs being adequate shelter. This
would be our home on wheels, RV, tent, or other living
space. In my opinion, the next most practical need is a
comfortable bed. Considering we spend a third of our lives
sleeping, having a decent bed is paramount to our health as
nomads.

We can debate whether comfort is actually a need or a
preference, but personally, I need to feel comfortable to
stay healthy, something many women share. My bed is a
24-inch wide wooden platform, and I sleep on 6 inches of
memory foam, with an added layer directly beneath me
that includes a folded sleeping bag and two soft blankets. I
have other multiple soft blankets piled on top, and all this
soft comfort has kept me warm and cozy on the coldest
winter nights in the desert. I sleep better swaddled in my
cocoon of blankets on my van bed than I ever did in a
regular bed in traditional housing!

Most women find comfort relevant to happiness, so make
sure to consider your own comfort levels planning your
nomadic life. How much space do you need? Can you
sleep comfortably on a cot or air mattress, or do you need a
more elaborate bed? I started out with a Coleman cot that
fell apart even before I got on the road … and decided the
more permanent platform bed would be less hassle. I've
since removed the platform bed, giving me more head

room to sit up, and making the van lighter. I use a piece of plywood for the bed base that just sits on the under-bed bins. The bins easily slide out and the memory foam on top of the plywood is more than adequate for comfort! I learned this bed set up from another female nomad!

Our human requirements are pretty basic, *but there are infinite ways our personal preferences shape how we meet those needs.* Our transition to nomadic life includes figuring out how to fulfill all the needs we had in a stick and brick dwelling ... shelter, food, waste removal, hygiene, community ... and to stay comfortable on the road.

Below is a list of needs to consider. This is by far not a comprehensive list, but will give you an idea of some of the decisions you'll face meeting your basic needs as a nomad:

Shelter: For wheeled nomads, this starts with vehicle, or rig. Will you be stealth camping, boondocking, or paying for campsites? Towing or not? How much room do you need to be comfortable but still live your dream? Will you need additional shelter like screen tents, tarps, or shade cloth?

Bed: Do you need a hard or soft mattress? Are you hardy, able to sleep on any surface, or more particular like me, feeling every lump and bump?

Water: Refillable water jugs, pump sprayers, or pump system built into vehicle.

Food: Storage in bins, coolers, fresh or shelf stable.

Cooking. Food storage, utensils. Special diet considerations.

Human waste: Urine and feces collection, storage and disposal. Much discussed everywhere there are nomad forums.

Hygiene: So many ways to accomplish this; wipes, spray bottles with soap and clean water, "top and bottom" bath, (also known as PPTA - Pussy/Pits/Tits and Ass) solar showers, camp showers, hand sanitizers, pump system (pesticide pump bottles used for water) pay for showers.

Temperature control: Fans, heaters, shade cloth, solar, AC, swamp coolers, following moderate climates.

Safety: Good safety habits, keys always accessible and in the same place, parking facing out, intuition, cell signal, SPOT device, or other means of getting help.

Along with getting our physical needs met, we'll need to determine personal emotional needs such as how isolated we want to be, how much communication with our tribe or family we need, whether we like traveling solo or in groups. A good part of this will evolve over time as your journey takes shape!

Once we've accomplished the basic physical set up, one of the most practical secrets to a successful and happy nomadic life is this:

Organize Everything!

It surprised me at the beginning of nomadic life how much longer it took to do the most routine things. There is SO. MUCH. MORE. WORK.

Depending on our set up, the lack of modern conveniences like running water, flush toilets and washing machines forces us to plan ahead for things we previously took for granted. We nomads are often viewed as carefree, *yet we spend more time, energy and effort than the average house dweller just to maintain our free nomadic life!*

The first night out in my van was overwhelming, with the first few months spent struggling up a very steep learning curve. While I can't guarantee you won't have the same experience, here are a few tips that might be helpful.

1. It is unbelievably easy to lose things in a tiny space!!! I swear it's easier to lose things in a van than in a house! Who knew! Have a place for every single thing in your van, and *put it back in the same place AS SOON AS YOU'RE DONE WITH IT!* You'll save untold hours of frustration with this method. DO NOT put something down and think you'll find it later!

2. Keep items you use daily, like toothbrush, toilet paper, meds, wipes, hand lotion, in one dedicated easily accessible area. You shouldn't have to fish through a bin to find your toothbrush every day. Keep frequently used items within reach and not in a bin covered by 3 other bins.

3. Arrange your storage so that the things you don't use often are tucked away. Don't waste time and energy continually moving things around to get to other things.

4. Organize items based on frequency of use. Store clothes you wear more often on top of other less worn clothing. I store my socks in one zippered plastic storage bag, and underwear and bras in another, saving time pawing through my clothes bin for those items.

5. Have an organized routine. My partner and I both start our day out with hot coffee and a simple breakfast, and I am a bear unless I get my coffee first thing. We've organized the kitchen so that everything we need in the morning is in one place ... coffee, filters, measuring spoon all go in one storage bag, the bag goes in the same place every day, and we only have to reach for the bag to start our mornings! I have the added benefit of being the late sleeper and a thoughtful partner who leaves it all laid out neatly on the table for me!

ADDENDUM: My partner and I now have separate kitchens and cooking areas. The individual organization is the same as described above. We find this is less stressful on our relationship, and helps our relationship thrive!

6. Get rid of as much stuff as you possibly can! Every nomad I've met has started out with too much stuff. I purged after four days on the road, and multiple times after that. It's impressive how much you can squeeze into a mini-van! How many forks and knives do we really need? How many coats, shoes or bras? Less clothing means faster visits at the laundromat. The fewer utensils, the less time cleaning. The more we can minimize, the more time and energy we'll have to enjoy our nomadic journey. Everything we carry must be handled, cared for and moved around, and *the less stuff we have, the more we live!* The goal is to ultimately have the least amount of stuff to accomplish all of the necessary life functions.

7. Planning and preparation are important, but also be prepared for mistakes! If you're anything like me, before you even get on the road, you'll have done what amounts to years of research looking at conversions, watching YouTube videos and making lists. No matter how much you've planned, it will all change once you start traveling! Once I got on the road, I dealt with the expected issues like how to manage my safety, but what affected me even more was not having a routine or organization that suited me.

8. Instead of dwelling on problems, solve them. Creative problem solving is probably one of the most essential skills of a nomad. Most women are natural problem solvers, we've been making the world go round behind the scenes since the beginning of civilization, but being out on the road, especially as a solo woman, can feel intimidating at times. Try to stay focused on solutions instead of problems, and learn to think outside of the box. Statistically, things always seem to work out. As Marianne Williamson says, *"Focus on the problem = faith in the problem. Focus on the solution = faith in possibility."*

The two most significant practical issues I had starting out was having too much stuff, and not having enough headroom over my bed! I designed the bed around the size of my storage bins, but I drastically underestimated how uncomfortable I would be not being able to sit up straight on my bed.

The pretty tapestry I'd hung on the ceiling gave me severe claustrophobia. The window curtains that I was so proud of sewing were super cute, but I had to fold and tuck and maneuver the reflectix around the curtains and cords, with ensuing frustration and swearing every single night. Alas, it all had to go. Now I pop my reflectix into my five van windows in a matter of minutes, with zero swearing.

The best-laid plans can go awry, and often do. When Nancy and I stealth camped in California, we couldn't make our morning coffee on the street. Neither one of us was set up to cook in our vans … we were used to boondocking on public land and setting up our outdoor kitchen for weeks at a time. We definitely were not organized for stealth camping. The Pacific Ocean was only a 15-minute drive which we LOVED, but we were miserable until we figured out the easiest way to get our coffee in the morning! We agreed that a few splurges on Starbucks was totally worth it, and eventually adjusted to waking up, driving to the beach first thing, and making our coffee there.

9. Remember to appreciate the present moment!
Remember your why from chapter one, and be sure to make time for rest and relaxation. Nomad life is not always about getting to the next place and seeing the next sight, sometimes it's about finding peace and being able to breathe and enjoy the scenery!

Nancy and I had a wild summer traveling our first year, mostly trying to get out of the heat of the Southwest while still staying within our gas budget. We saw some fantastic places, making a circuit from Flagstaff AZ, across the Mohave to the Sequoia National Forest in California, on to the Pacific Ocean, and then back to Flagstaff, all in about 3 months.

We were on a huge learning curve. Wanting to avoid the Monsoons in Flagstaff, we headed into California, but were unprepared for the ungodly heat in the lower elevations. It was 117 degrees when we crossed the Mohave, and we were forced by the heat to find a motel. Not knowing the area we landed in, we stayed in what I'm convinced was a gang-run motel in a town-from-hell, which will here remain unnamed! When we finally made it to a dispersed camping area, it was still 100 degrees!

Thankfully we were graciously guided by an experienced nomad to a gorgeous area up in the Sequoia National Forest, higher in elevation and much cooler, which also, unfortunately, had zero cell coverage. The only cell signal was up on a vast rock formation that overlooked thousands of miles of primal forest, a short drive down the dirt road and then an easy 10-minute hike up the hill. I was still trying to resolve the motor vehicle relocation mess, and I hiked up the rock frequently, to repeatedly experience aggravating phone calls to my insurance company, dropped calls, and long unproductive holds with Motor Vehicles. I let myself get distraught over the whole thing, and found myself *CRYING and COMPLAINING*, while surrounded by the most breathtaking views, literally in our backyard, of the Sequoia National Forest. Nancy wasn't in much better shape. Thankfully we came to our senses, consciously shifted our focus, and spent the rest of our time there reveling in the incredible natural vista surrounding us.

Facing the challenges of nomadic living, and the utter confusion that can sometimes happen, can be a fortuitous time to discover how well we know ourselves.

Living a simple life stripped of modern distractions can be a gift to our soul, a window to our deepest desires, and a chance to create an authentic life lived with joy. Learning to live without, we invite in the richness of life.

Once I was on the road for a while, I discovered my likes and dislikes, and how to be happy as a nomad. I found I don't mind traveling, but I also need a place to settle, at least for a few weeks, where I can get some rest. Personally, I need to be connected online, so checkboxes for a happy camp includes a cell signal, a local library, a flat space and shade for yoga and meditation, and an abundance of privacy and quiet.

Most nomads are creative souls, making it vital for our mental health to continue to follow our creative urges once we're on the road. I find it rare to encounter a bored nomad, most of us have a variety of creative interests that more than fill our downtime. Mine include playing my guitar, writing and journaling, reading, beading, talking to friends and family back east, yoga, and meditation. I need lots of  quality time with my partner Nancy, balanced by regular solitary time for contemplation. I can get pretty grouchy and out of sorts if I can't get those needs met, and having space for my guitar, journals, books, crystals, beading supplies, and a yoga mat is a priority for my health and happiness.

If we're to have balanced, healthy lives living as nomads, it's important to make joy, rest and relaxation a priority, or else why are we even doing this?

As far as other practical advice, I've found these to be invaluable:

Have a backup plan ... or two!!!!

Don't be nice. The "nice woman" role doesn't serve us well as nomads.

Put up a tent! It can mark your space when you're out, and define the boundaries of your camp.

If you're a solo nomad, put out two chairs.

Don't display your valuables to anyone.

Lock up at night.

Don't sleep naked when you're stealth camping!

Most of all, revel in your freedom!

I hope this book has imparted a feeling of hope, determination, and encouragement to accompany you on your way as a Wild Woman Nomad!

Read on to Dig Deeper for this chapter, living your "ideal day" as a nomad.

I'll leave you with these blessed words from Mary Oliver:

The Summer Day

Who made the world?

Who made the swan, and the black bear?

189

Who made the grasshopper? This grasshopper, I mean- the one who has flung herself out of the grass, the one who is eating sugar out of my hand, who is moving her jaws back and forth instead of up and down- who is gazing around with her enormous and complicated eyes.

Now she lifts her pale forearms and thoroughly washes her face. Now she snaps her wings open, and floats away.

I don't know exactly what a prayer is.

I do know how to pay attention, how to fall down into the grass, how to kneel down in the grass, how to be idle and blessed, how to stroll through the fields, which is what I have been doing all day.

Tell me, what else should I have done?

Doesn't everything die at last, and too soon?

Tell me, what is it you plan to do with your one wild and precious life? —Mary Oliver

DIG DEEPER: MAKE PLANS FOR YOUR IDEAL DAY AS A NOMAD

"On a profound level, and in a very real way, imagination and creativity leads us back to our Wild Woman self, into the life-giving depths of our soul."
Mary Ellen Telesha, Life Coach

We've already done the Ideal Day exercise in Chapter Four, but this time we'll be looking for *practical* ideas that come up as you imagine your perfect, ideal day as a Wild Woman Nomad.

The Ideal Day Exercise.

The ideal day exercise is a chance to let your imagination take you into your future. To start, allow yourself to enter into a daydream about your perfect day as a nomad.

Imagine waking up in the morning on your ideal day. When you open your eyes, what do you see? Where are you? What do you see out the window? Who's with you?

Are you in a vehicle, tent, RV? What are the specifics? What does your bed look like?

How do you go to the bathroom and deal with your waste?

You'll be getting ready for breakfast - where do you prepare your breakfast? What are you having for breakfast? Now imagine - where do you sit and have your breakfast? Where are all your cooking and eating utensils stored?

After breakfast, you'll probably have some kind of hygiene routine. Where do you store your hygiene items, like toothbrush, washcloth, soap?

What's next in your ideal day?

Go through a complete day from morning to bedtime, and imagine as many **practical** details about this perfect day in your ideal life as you can think of.

How is it going to feel when you're traveling?

How is your living space organized?

Are there situations that come up that require some problem-solving?

Make sure to make a note of any specifics you notice. Instead of worrying about your future, **become the creatrix of your future!**

"When you imagine what you've wanted, you've already FELT the feeling you want by imagining it! Accept the moment of yearning as real now, it's a memory of the future! Maps drawn in yearning always take you to heart's desires if you remain in the truth of who you are." ~ Martha Beck

RESOURCES

(This is a list of links to some nomadic resources for women. This is by no means a comprehensive list, but a jumping-off point for your own research. If you're reading the print version of this book, they can be found by googling each title.)

Not in alphabetical order.

CosmicNomadVoyager.com. My van life website. Facebook page. https://www.facebook.com/CosmicNomadVoyager/ Instagram: Cosmic Nomad Voyager

Cheap RV living. Bob Wells. Website. https://www.cheaprvliving.com/ Cheap RV living. YouTube Channel and Facebook.

Homes On Wheels Alliance. (HOWA) Homesonwheelsalliance.org

Bob Witham. You Tube.

Debra Dickinson. YouTube

Robert Witham Book. How to be a Nomad. http://robertwitham.com/store/how-to-be-a-nomad/

HOWA Facebook group. Search Home On Wheels Alliance on Facebook.

Fabulous RVing Women FRVW. Facebook Group.
https://www.facebook.com/groups/491667721166003/

Solo Female Vanlife. Facebook Group.
https://www.facebook.com/groups/solofemalevanlife/

Simple RV living for women. Facebook Group.
https://www.facebook.com/groups/719191994765778/

Minivan Campers and Dwellers. Facebook Group.
https://www.facebook.com/groups/1114130071995531/

LGBT Nomads. Facebook Group.
https://www.facebook.com/groups/LGBTnomadics/

Martha Beck. Website. https://marthabeck.com/

Martha Beck Institute. Website.
https://marthabeckinstitute.com/

Escapees. Website. https://www.escapees.com/

RVing Women. RVW Website.
https://www.rvingwomen.org/

DEFINITIONS

Black Tank: Holding tank for toilet waste.

BLM: Bureau of Land Management. A federal agency that administers more than 247.3 million acres of public land, mostly in the Western part of the U.S. BLM is also used to describe the land itself. i.e., "I'm camping on the BLM."

Body Compass: Internal guidance system expressed by sensations in the body. (See Chapter Three.)

Boondocking: Camping or Vehicle dwelling in an area that doesn't provide water, waste removal, or electricity. Often free.

Build: Usually referred to customizing vehicles for nomadic use. Conversion of a vehicle into a living space.

Conversion Van: A van in which the cargo space has been converted to a special purpose, such as a living space. A cargo van that is sent to third-party companies to be outfitted with various luxuries for vandwelling.

Dispersed camping: Free camping in National Forests, outside of developed paid campgrounds, usually with none to little amenities.

Dry camping: Camping in a location where electric/water/sewer connections are not available at each site.

Gray Tank: Holding tank for dirty water from showers/sink. Not human waste.

Hookups: Services in a campground such as electricity, water, waste that directly connect to a vehicle/RV. Paid services also can be found at truck stops.

LTVA: Long Term Visitor Area. Special permit areas, non-developed camping areas with limited facilities on BLM land in the West.

Nomad: Someone who travels and/or lives without living in a fixed dwelling.

Reflectix: A reflective insulation that looks like silver covered bubble wrap. Commonly used by nomads. Custom cut and put in windows to reflect heat, insulate, and provide stealth.

RTR: Rubber Tramp Rendezvous. Annual Gathering of Nomads originally founded by Bob Wells, organized by HOWA.

RV: Recreational Vehicle. Usually refers to Class A, Class B, or Class C recreational vehicles.

Schoolie: A school bus converted into an RV.

Shade Cloth: A stretch of fabric normally draped over greenhouses to ensure they remain cool. Used by nomads for cooling in hot, sunny climates.

S.P.O.T. communication device: A handheld GPS satellite device not dependent on cell signal. Mainly used to notify rescue officials in the event of an emergency, but paid monthly plans include other services.

Stealth Camping/parking: Parking overnight in an area not designated for camping, usually on a street or parking lot.

Sticks and Bricks: Traditional housing. House, Apartment, Condo.

Swamp cooler: An evaporative cooler (also swamp box, desert cooler and wet air cooler) A device that cools air through the evaporation of water.

Vandweller: A personal living either part-time or full-time in a van.

W.I.G.: Wildly Improbable Goals. (See Chapter One.)

WRTR: Annual gathering of women nomads, originally directed by Suanne Carlson and now organized by her through HOWA.

Made in United States
Troutdale, OR
05/06/2024

19686756R00110